First World War
and Army of Occupation
War Diary
France, Belgium and Germany

40 DIVISION
119 Infantry Brigade
South Wales Borderers
12th Battalion
1 June 1916 - 16 February 1918

WO95/2606/6

The Naval & Military Press Ltd
www.nmarchive.com
Published in association with The National Archives

Published by

The Naval & Military Press Ltd

Unit 10 Ridgewood Industrial Park,

Uckfield, East Sussex,

TN22 5QE England

Tel: +44 (0) 1825 749494

www.naval-military-press.com

www.nmarchive.com

This diary has been reprinted in facsimile from the original. Any imperfections are inevitably reproduced and the quality may fall short of modern type and cartographic standards.

© Crown Copyright
Images reproduced by permission of The National Archives, London, England, 2015.

Contents

Document type	Place/Title	Date From	Date To
Heading	WO95/2606/6 12 Battalion South Wales Borderers		
Heading	40th Division 119th Infy Bde 12th Bn Sth Wales Bordrs Jun 1916 Jan 1918		
Heading	119th Brigade. 40th Division. Battalion Went out to France With 119th Brigade 40th Division-Landing At Havre 2.6.16 12th Battalion South Wales Borderers Jun 1916		
Heading	War Diary Of The 12th (S) Battn. South Wales Borderer From 1st June 1916 Volume 1		
War Diary	Southampton	01/06/1916	01/06/1916
War Diary	Havre And Sanvic	02/06/1916	02/06/1916
War Diary	Sanvic	03/06/1916	03/06/1916
War Diary	Bourecq	04/06/1916	12/06/1916
War Diary	Bourecq & Houchin	13/06/1916	13/06/1916
War Diary	Houchin	14/06/1916	14/06/1916
War Diary	A&B& HQ Calonne	14/06/1916	14/06/1916
War Diary	Calonne	15/06/1916	18/06/1916
War Diary	Houchin	19/06/1916	20/06/1916
War Diary	Houchin & Calonne	21/06/1916	21/06/1916
War Diary	Calonne	22/06/1916	24/06/1916
War Diary	Houchin	24/06/1916	25/06/1916
War Diary	Marle Les Mines	26/06/1916	30/06/1916
War Diary	Blackdowry	01/06/1916	01/06/1916
Heading	119th Brigade. 40th Division. 12th Battalion South Wales Borderers July 1916		
War Diary	Marle Les Mines	01/07/1916	02/07/1916
War Diary	D & Barlin	03/07/1916	03/07/1916
War Diary	Calonne	04/07/1916	15/07/1916
War Diary	Bully Grenay	16/07/1916	19/07/1916
War Diary	Calonne	20/07/1916	22/07/1916
War Diary	Lesbrebis	23/07/1916	30/07/1916
War Diary	Calonne.	31/07/1916	31/07/1916
Heading	119th Brigade. 40th Division. 12th Battalion South Wales Borderers August 1916		
War Diary	Calonne	01/08/1916	16/08/1916
War Diary	Les Brebis	17/08/1916	23/08/1916
War Diary	Loos	24/08/1916	28/08/1916
War Diary	Maroc	29/08/1916	31/08/1916
Heading	119th Brigade. 40th Division. 12th Battalion South Wales Borderers September 1916		
War Diary	Loos	01/09/1916	10/09/1916
War Diary	Les Brebis	11/09/1916	18/09/1916
War Diary	Maroc Left	19/09/1916	30/09/1916
Heading	119th Brigade. 40th Division. 12th South Wales Borderers October 1916		
War Diary	Maroc	01/10/1916	19/10/1916
War Diary	Maroc Loos.	20/10/1916	21/10/1916
War Diary	Loos.	22/10/1916	29/10/1916
War Diary	Les Brebis.	30/10/1916	31/10/1916

Heading	119th Brigade. 40th Division. 12th Battalion South Wales Borderers November 1916		
War Diary	Bruay	01/11/1916	01/11/1916
War Diary	Monchy Breton.	02/11/1916	02/11/1916
War Diary	Monts-En-Ternas.	03/11/1916	04/11/1916
War Diary	Bonnieres.	05/11/1916	05/11/1916
War Diary	Autheux.	06/11/1916	15/11/1916
War Diary	Fortel.	16/11/1916	17/11/1916
War Diary	Bonnieres	18/11/1916	18/11/1916
War Diary	Bouquemaison.	18/11/1916	22/11/1916
War Diary	Beauval.	23/11/1916	23/11/1916
War Diary	St. Leger	24/11/1916	24/11/1916
War Diary	Buigny-Les-Abbee	25/11/1916	25/11/1916
War Diary	Buigny.	26/11/1916	26/11/1916
War Diary	Pont Remy	26/11/1916	30/11/1916
Heading	119th Brigade. 40th Division. 12th Battalion South Wales Borderers December 1916		
War Diary	Pont Remy.	01/12/1916	31/12/1916
Heading	119th Brigade. 40th Division. 12th Battalion South Wales Borderers January 1917		
War Diary	Laurepas Ravine.	01/01/1917	03/01/1917
War Diary	Camp 21	04/01/1917	14/01/1917
War Diary	Asquith Flats.	15/01/1917	31/01/1917
Heading	119th Brigade. 40th Division. 12th Battalion South Wales Borderers February 1917		
War Diary	Saillye Laurette.	01/02/1917	10/02/1917
War Diary	Camp 21	11/02/1917	28/02/1917
Heading	119th Brigade. 40th Division. 12th Battalion South Wales Borderers March 1917		
War Diary	Belair.	01/03/1917	09/03/1917
War Diary	Clery	10/03/1917	20/03/1917
War Diary	Camp 21	21/03/1917	25/03/1917
War Diary	Little Dale Barrack	26/03/1917	31/03/1917
Heading	119th Brigade 40th Division. 12th Battalion South Wales Borderers April 1917		
War Diary	Littledale Barracks.	01/04/1917	09/04/1917
War Diary	Etricourt.	10/04/1917	20/04/1917
War Diary	Queens Cross.	21/04/1917	23/04/1917
War Diary	Gouzea-Court.	24/04/1917	30/04/1917
Heading	119th Brigade 40th Division. 12th Battalion South Wales Borderers May 1917		
War Diary	A Vacqueris	01/05/1917	31/05/1917
Heading	119th Brigade 40th Division. 12th Battalion South Wales Borderers June 1917		
War Diary	Dessart Wood.	01/06/1917	02/06/1917
War Diary	Villers Plouich	03/06/1917	09/06/1917
War Diary	Caesar's Camp	10/06/1917	19/06/1917
War Diary	Dessart Wood.	20/06/1917	26/06/1917
War Diary	Gonnel-/Ieu	27/06/1917	30/06/1917
Heading	119th Brigade 40th Division. 12th Battalion South Wales Borderers July 1917		
War Diary	Gonnelieu	01/07/1917	31/07/1917
Heading	119th Brigade 40th Division. 12th Battalion South Wales Borderers August 1917		
Heading	War Diary 12th (S) Bn. South Wales Borderers August 1917		

War Diary	Gonnelieu.	01/08/1917	31/08/1917
Heading	119th Brigade 40th Division. 12th Battalion South Wales Borderers September 1917		
Heading	War Diary 12th S Bn South Wales Borderers September 1917		
War Diary	Gouzeaucourt	01/09/1917	15/09/1917
War Diary	Gonnelieu	16/09/1917	23/09/1917
War Diary	Gouzeaucourt.	24/09/1917	30/09/1917
Heading	119th Brigade 40th Division. 12th Battalion South Wales Borderers October 1917		
Heading	War Diary 12th (S) Bn South Wales Borderers October 1917		
War Diary	Gonnelieu	01/10/1917	07/10/1917
War Diary	Heudecourt.	07/10/1917	08/10/1917
War Diary	Doingt.	09/10/1917	10/10/1917
War Diary	Gouy-En-Artois.	11/10/1917	28/10/1917
War Diary	Humber-Court.	29/10/1917	31/10/1917
Heading	119th Brigade 40th Division. 12th Battalion South Wales Borderers November 1917		
Heading	War Diary 12th (S) Bn South Wales Borderers November 1917		
War Diary	Humbercourt	01/11/1917	15/11/1917
War Diary	Gouy.	16/11/1917	16/11/1917
War Diary	Gommiecourtz	17/11/1917	18/11/1917
War Diary	Barastre	19/11/1917	20/11/1917
War Diary	Doignes.	21/11/1917	21/11/1917
War Diary	Gaincourt	22/11/1917	22/11/1917
War Diary	Bourlon Wood.	23/11/1917	25/11/1917
War Diary	Lechelle Berles-Aux-Bois	26/11/1917	27/11/1917
War Diary	Berles-Aux-Bois.	28/11/1917	30/11/1917
Heading	119th Brigade 40th Division. 12th Battalion South Wales Borderers December 1917		
Heading	War Diary 12th (S) Bn. South Wales Borderers Dec 1917		
War Diary	Berles-Au-Bois Ervillers	01/12/1917	02/12/1917
War Diary	Railway Reserve	03/12/1917	06/12/1917
War Diary	Bullecourt Sector	08/12/1917	14/12/1917
War Diary	Ervillers	15/12/1917	20/12/1917
War Diary	Bullecourt	21/12/1917	26/12/1917
War Diary	Railway Reserve	27/12/1917	31/12/1917
Heading	119th Brigade 40th Division. 12th Battalion South Wales Borderers January 1918		
Heading	War Diary 12th Bn S W Borderers January 1918		
War Diary	Railway Reserve.	01/01/1918	01/01/1918
War Diary	Bullecourt	02/01/1918	05/01/1918
War Diary	Mory.	06/01/1918	08/01/1918
War Diary	Bullecourt	09/01/1918	13/01/1918
War Diary	Railway Reserve.	14/01/1918	17/01/1918
War Diary	Bullecourt	19/01/1918	21/01/1918
War Diary	Mory.	22/01/1918	25/01/1918
War Diary	Bullecourt	26/01/1918	29/01/1918
War Diary	Railway Reserve.	30/01/1918	31/01/1918
Heading	119th Brigade. 40th Division. Battalion Became Part Of 9th Entrenching Battalion 16.2.18 12th Battalion South Wales Borderers February 1918		
War Diary	Railway Reserve.	01/02/1918	02/02/1918

War Diary	Bullecourt.	03/02/1918	06/02/1918
War Diary	Mary	07/02/1918	09/02/1918
War Diary	Bellacourt	10/02/1918	16/02/1918

WO95/2606/6

12 Battalion South Wales Borderers

40TH DIVISION
119TH INFY BDE

12TH BN STH WALES BORDRS

JUN 1916-JAN 1918

DISBANDED

2606

119th Brigade.
40th Division.

Battalion went out to France with 119th Brigade
40th Division - landing at HAVRE 2.6.16

12th BATTALION

SOUTH WALES BORDERERS

JUNE 1916.

12 S. W(o)ers. R.
vol 1
June
119/40

XL

Confidential

War Diary
of
The 12th (S) Batt" South Wales Borderers

From 1st June 1916.

Volume 1

[Stamp: 12TH SERVICE BATTALION (3rd GWENT) SOUTH WALES BORDERERS 30 JUN 1916]

Army Form C. 2118

WAR DIARY
or
INTELLIGENCE SUMMARY
(Erase heading not required.)

Instructions regarding War Diaries and Intelligence Summaries are contained in F. S. Regs., Part II. and the Staff Manual respectively. Title Pages will be prepared in manuscript.

Place	Date 1916	Hour	Summary of Events and Information	Remarks and references to Appendices
Southampton	June 1		The Battalion sailed to HAVRE at 7 o'clock this evening arriving at 3 o'clock next morning.	
HAVRE and SANVIC	June 2nd		We marched off the boat at 4.30 o'clock to SANVIC no 2 camp, where we arrived at 10 o'clock. The road up was very hilly, and the weather very hot, but the men came along very well and no one fell out. The rest of the day was devoted to resting the men. The C.O. was O.C. Troops on the boat, and issued orders at 9 o'clock p.m.	
SANVIC	June 3rd		The Battalion marched out of Camp at 8.30 am, leaving "D" Company to follow on at 11 o'clock. We entrained at HAVRE for LILLERS, at which place we arrived at 5.15 am the next morning.	
DOURCQ	June 4th		Lieut R. Symes went forward as Billeting Officer, and when we arrived at DOURECQ at 8 am. we found Billets waiting for us. The men were Billeted in Barns and Lofts, and when straw had been procured were comfortable. Officers Billets were in houses, nearly all had beds and seemed to be excellent. DOURECQ is on the main road from AIRE to LILLERS, and as many General Officers passed through particular attention had to be paid to saluting and the smartness of the men.	
DOURCQ	June 5th		The men were exercised in rapid loading, Physical training and Gas Helmet practice.	
DOURECQ	June 6th		The C.O. held an inspection of companies in marching Order. The arrangements for meals are as follows. The field Kitchens are packed with the transport & sent down to each coy H.Q. at meal times, with the tea or cooked ration. By this means, the Sergt Cook is enabled to supervise the cooking, and the horses get exercised in going to and fro	

Army Form C. 2118

WAR DIARY
or
INTELLIGENCE SUMMARY
(Erase heading not required.)

Instructions regarding War Diaries and Intelligence Summaries are contained in F. S. Regs., Part II. and the Staff Manual respectively. Title Pages will be prepared in manuscript.

Place	Date 1916	Hour	Summary of Events and Information	Remarks and references to Appendices
BOURECQ	June 6th 7th 8th		Training in gas Helmet practice, Physical training, rapid loading, carried out. Companies bathed in a stream which runs through BOURECQ. When Rations were carried today. Company training was carried out. MG	
"	9th		The Battalion went a Route march of about 11 miles starting at 9.30am via LILLERS. BURBURE. EGURDECRUES. LESPESSES. BOURECQ. The weather was fine and hot; no men fell out, but the road is very trying to the feet. We arrived back in BOURECQ at 1.15pm. MG	
"	11th		Church Parade was held in the transport field at 10.30am, the Revd Rev Thomas took the service. MG	
"	12th		Company training was carried out and all Officers + N.C.O's attended a lecture and demonstration on Gas Helmets at ST HILAIRE. Heavy Thunderstorm cut the lecture short. MG	
BOURECQ to HOUCHIN	13th		Companies bathed + did Company training, weather cold and showery. The Battalion marched out of BOURECQ at 8am for HOUCHIN en route for the trenches. 2nd/Lt F P ENRIGHT having to go on a course + 2nd/Lt O.P. Taylor with 9 men went left behind. Machinegun Shells were carried on a G.S. wagon sent by the Division. They also left their supplies kit of underwear also their cardigans. MG We arrived at HOUCHIN at 4pm. The route was deep in mud + very inclement, Tea was served at 5.30 and eights out at 9.30. Kept we could wear plainly hear the enemy machineguns, rifles &c, the whole day was very wet all the time. MG	
HOUCHIN	14th		The Battalion marched out of HOUCHIN at 9.30 am to BULLY GRENAY via NOEX-LES-MINES + PETIT SAINS, as the last named the siege Helmets	

WAR DIARY or INTELLIGENCE SUMMARY

Army Form C. 2118

Place	Date 1916	Hour	Summary of Events and Information	Remarks and references to Appendices
HOUCHIN	June 14th		which had been shelled at HOUCHIN we set out, as the whole of the road from here to BULLY GRENAY is periodically shelled. The Bn also advanced by Coys at 20 yards interval, all the evening from NOEX-LES-MINES shows signs of having been heavily shelled. We reached BULLY GRENAY at 10 p.m. the 1st Bn S.W.B. interviewed us for lunch. At 2.30 p.m. the companies reported to the Trenches. H.Q. and A & B Coys were attached to 1st S.W.B. and C & D companies under Major C.B. Hone, to 2nd Bn Welsh Regt. The companies took their places man by man with the other Bns & specialist officers were attached to their corresponding members. Both Bns were very kind in giving all information possible as to carrying on and in entertaining us as men. We were in the CALONNE section extending from PIT PROP CORNER to CALONNE ALLEY (C & D companies with the left cut section of the sector (2nd Welsh) His	
A, B & H.Q. CALONNE			to them	
CALONNE	June 15th		The Brigade is the 3rd and all reports were received by the B" to which we were attached. Details are not exactly obtainable as I went in to the first casualty occurred to day. No 35387 Pte Edmunds was killed by a trench mortar falling on top of a dug out. The situation was quiet all day with intermittent trench mortar and artillery fire on both sides. The same day No 24182 Pte Ivy a machine gunner was killed through a trench mortar falling on this dug out.	
CALONNE	June 16th		a quiet day with no casualties	
" " "	17th		still quiet, minor news round from N to N.E., one O.R. casualty (killed)	*
" " "	18th		Three men killed to day by trench mortar fire and two wounded. To day we marched out of the trenches leaving the line as follows:—	*

WAR DIARY
or
INTELLIGENCE SUMMARY

(Erase heading not required.)

Army Form C. 2118

Instructions regarding War Diaries and Intelligence Summaries are contained in F.S. Regs., Part II. and the Staff Manual respectively. Title Pages will be prepared in manuscript.

Place	Date 1916	Hour	Summary of Events and Information	Remarks and references to Appendices
CALONNE	June 18th		Nos. 1 and 2 Platoons at 12.30 p.m. " 3 and 4 " " 12.40 p.m. " 5 and 6 " " 12.50 p.m. " 7 and 8 " " 1 p.m. A halt was made at BULLY GRENAY, where dinners were served in the square and the other half Battalion served up. The Battalion then proceeded by companies at 200 yards interval, to HOUCHIN, arriving there at 5pm. The men marched well & were commended by Col. 119th I.L. Brigade Staff as the way they came in afresh in after ten + days in the trenches. MB	
HOUCHIN	June 19th		The whole of today was spent in cleaning up, washing &c. MB	
HOUCHIN	20th		Inspections of Kit, ammunition, Rations & clothes, were carried out, and all deficiencies remedied as far as possible. The Companies were also inspected by the C.O. "A" Coy bathed in the evening at the Baths here, but owing to a breakdown in the pumping arrangements the other companies could not bathe. The weather for the last few days has been bright & warm. MB	
HOUCHIN & CALONNE	June 21st		The "B" marched out of HOUCHIN at 8.30 for CALONNE by the same route as on the 14th inst proceeding by companies at 200 yards distance all the way. Dinners were served at the Chateau at BULLY GRENAY, and at 11pm the "B" moved off by platoons at 200 yds interval. "A" & "B" Coys & 2 Lewis machine guns with 4 attached to 1st B/D minster Regt on the right of the CALONNE SECTOR. Work done to the 1st B/D Gloucester Regt on the left of the CALONNE SECTOR. Work done this night consisted of wiring the front line, general repairs & cleaning up. Our H.E. Howitzers engaged enemy trench mortar as M 20 b 4 4 and over as in T.M. engaged enemy M.M. at M and had direct hits, our sources claimed a hit. MB	

1375 Wt. W 593/826 1,000,000 4/15 J.B.C. & A. A.D.S.S./Forms/C. 2118.

WAR DIARY or INTELLIGENCE SUMMARY

Army Form C. 2118

(Erase heading not required.)

Instructions regarding War Diaries and Intelligence Summaries are contained in F.S. Regs, Part II and the Staff Manual respectively. Title Pages will be prepared in manuscript.

Place	Date 1916	Hour	Summary of Events and Information	Remarks and references to Appendices
CALONNE	June 22nd		Warm bright day. There was a very slight gas wind. There was almost a total absence of any sort of firing during the day & night. A Soldier (Kemp) coming into a dug out on a baking state, accidentally shot another man, the bullet who died shortly after. Today the Highland Regiment (Black watch) relieved the 1st Gordons in this sector. WG	
CALONNE	June 23rd		Everything very quiet with the exception of some trench mortar fire on our side which was hardly replied to by the enemy. Very severe thunderstorm in the afternoon which flooded many of the trenches and flooded out our temporary Orderly Room. WG	
CALONNE	June 24th		We were relieved at 9.30 am to make way for the 2th B&n Suffolk Regt. who were relieved near LES DREBIS & we arrived at HOUCHIN camp at 5pm. Tea was then served & the men rested. About 11pm there was a scare of Hostile aircraft and all lights went out — but no one saw anything exactly. Thundery weather. WG	
HOUCHIN	June 25th		The morning was devoted to cleaning up and an inspection. At 2.30pm the B&n marched out to MARLE-LES-MINES. The were very comfortable. WG	
"	"			
MARLE LES MINES	June 26th		The day was devoted to bay cleaning & bathing at AUCHEL Baths, weather fine & warm with occasional showers. Extraordinary that the extraordinary amount of literature now being issued — the no of returns so far in excess of that at Home. Stationery Box issued at home is very different from the amount of stationery required. One suffers very much from indigestion of orders. WG	
"	June 27		The B&n was employed in cleaning up for an inspection tomorrow & C.O. inspected all Coys in marching Order. Sunday our badge was issued, a strip of green cloth one inch wide worn at the top of the sleeve by the Shoulder, arranged today. WG	
"	June 28th		The G.O.C. 119 Inf Brigade inspected the B&n by Coys in the morning, & expressed himself as very well pleased with the steadiness & smartness of the men.	

1875. Wt. W593/825. 1,000,000. 4/15. J.B.C. & A. A.D.S.S./Forms/C. 2118.

Army Form C. 2118

WAR DIARY
or
INTELLIGENCE SUMMARY

(Erase heading not required.)

Instructions regarding War Diaries and Intelligence Summaries are contained in F. S. Regs., Part II. and the Staff Manual respectively. Title Pages will be prepared in manuscript.

Place	Date	Hour	Summary of Events and Information	Remarks and references to Appendices
MARLE LES MINES	June 1916 28		The rest of the day was devoted to Company training, weather overshowery.	
	29		weather fine & warm. The Bn route marched to Peines returning in the evening. The bombing officers two detachments of C. by through training with live bombs.	
"	30		Company training was carried on all day, weather fine.	

Alexander ?
Lieut. Colonel,
Comdg. 12th Bn. South Wales Borderers.

1375 Wt. W593/826 1,000,000 4/15 J.B.C. & A. A.D.S.S./Forms/C. 2118.

WAR DIARY or INTELLIGENCE SUMMARY

Army Form C. 2118

Place	Date	Hour	Summary of Events and Information	Remarks and references to Appendices
Blackdown Junction	1916		The Battn. entrained at Frimley Station for SOUTHAMPTON at a strength of 34 officers and 992 other ranks. The names of the Officers who accompanied the Battalion are as under:—	

Lieut Colonel G.A. Pope Commanding. Major G.B. Hone 2nd-in-command.
Captain W.G. Brown Adjutant. Lieut & QMr J. Abbott. Lieut R.J. Buckham Transport Officer.

"A" Coy.
Captn. E.A. Whitworth O.C.
" J.W. Foreman 2nd in comd.
Lieut H.R. Taylor
2/ " H.S. Edmonds
" " W.J. Proctor
" " H.P. Enright

"B" Coy.
Captn. B.F. Murphy O.C.
" R.A. Godwin-Austen 2nd ,,
Lieut H.C. Lloyd
" " A.E. Elborn
" " J.R.W. Taylor
" " J.E. Reeves.

"C" Coy.
Captn. H.C. Rees O.C.
" Con. Pritchard 2nd comd.
Lieut W.E.G. Howell
" O.P. Taylor
" E.H. Francis
" J.D. Vickers

"D" Coy.
Captn. C.C. Hoffmeister O.C.
Lieut O.D. Nixon 2nd comd
2/ " I.M. Renwick
Lieut V.S.O. Jones
2/ " H.R. Jones
2/ " H.J. Brown

Supernumerary Officers
Lieut J.R. Symes
" J.S. Lewis
" A. Newman
" S.R. Williams
" D. Elward R.A.M.C. (M.O.)

Lieut H.R. Taylor was sent on in advance as advance officer.

119th Brigade.
40th Division.

12th BATTALION

SOUTH WALES BORDERERS

JULY 1916.

40 July
July 1916
12 S.W. Borderers

2 X
13 sheets

12TH Bn S.W.BORDERERS   B486

Army Form C. 2118

WAR DIARY
or
INTELLIGENCE SUMMARY
(Erase heading not required.)

Instructions regarding War Diaries and Intelligence Summaries are contained in F. S. Regs., Part II. and the Staff Manual respectively. Title Pages will be prepared in manuscript.

Place	Date 1916	Hour	Summary of Events and Information	Remarks and references to Appendices
MARLE LES MINES	July 1st		The Battalion carried on Company training in the morning, & has out some bombing practice in the afternoon, and unfortunately Private A. Newman was accidentally killed by a bomb being dropped by the weapon. Captain J. Newman was slightly injured. Pte A. Newman was an exceedingly keen and able Officer. He acted as Bombing Officer, and carried out his duties with care, skill and thoroughness almost unrivalled. He was a favourite with everyone and his loss is greatly felt. The Intelligence reports note that we have carried on without today at 9.30 a.m. Weather fine & warm.	
D.O.	July 2nd		Sunday Church Parade in the morning, at 6.15 p.m. Lt Newman was buried, his Platoon formed the firing party, 'C' Company attended as mourners, and all the officers including G.O.C. 119th Brigade. The Brigade Band played the Dead March to the cemetery, and the whole affair was very impressive. The Revd. Rev. Thomas conducted the service. Capt. Morgan reported at 4 p.m. getting more the worse for his accident.	
D.o & BARLIN	July 3rd		The morning was devoted to packing up & cleaning up Billets, as 4 p.m. we marched out to BARLIN with 18th R.W.F. Major C.B. Hoare being in command of the Half Brigade. The C.O. and Captain Reid went up to the trenches to reconnoitre the line. We arrived at BARLIN at 6.15 p.m. owing to a mistake our Billeting was not ready, and it was 10 p.m. before the Companies were arranged for. The Billets in BARLIN are very filthy and there is no latrine accommodation to speak of. The section moved at 9.30 a.m. after waging an unequal war with countless bugs. At noon we marched off for the trenches to BULLY GRENAY, arriving at HERSIN at 4 p.m., after dividing at HERSIN. It proved from 2 p.m. on and the roads were slippery, so the 110th Division were relieving the 1st from PETIT SAINS, we advanced by Platoons at 5 minutes	

WAR DIARY
or
INTELLIGENCE SUMMARY
(Erase heading not required.)

Army Form C. 2118

Place	Date	Hour	Summary of Events and Information	Remarks and references to Appendices
CALONNE	July 1916 4TH		Inward, and the sky being cloudy no balloons were up & we were not shelled. We relieved the 10th Gloucesters in the CALONNE SECTION. Left sub sector with the 19th Batt on our Right. The Relief was completed at 4pm without incident - 2 TMs were exchanged. G.	
"	JULY 5TH		At 12.30pm all 3 companies sent out patrols & wiring parties. Two German wiring parties were observed at M.15.c. Between 5 & 6pm. our Stokes guns opened fire on retaliation for enemy T.M. fires and our aerial torpedoes also fired at and silenced enemy Minenwerfer, which had been firing in the centre Coy. This Mortar was reported to be at M.16.c.d.9.5. Was on the front line was straightened and general clearing of the trenches was carried out. G.	
	JULY 6TH		The enemy proved very active with Trench mortars and artillery fire and rendered a large portion of "D" Coy (left Coy) line untenable. A raid went out from Sap F at 11pm & proved everything. Trial of M.26.a.4.5. About 8pm the enemy sent over 50 rounds of Trifle explosive 5.9 and 6 aerial torpedoes which landed close to B.O.Y.A.V.21. Work done by wiring parties, and draining after the very wet weather. G.	
	JULY 7TH		We were relieved at 4pm by 18th B. Welch Regt. The relief was completed without incident at 5.15pm. We went into support at CALONNE. The men are billetted in cellars and are very comfortable. Aboves enough our Lewis machine guns in the support line were very active and also the heavy Artillery.	

WAR DIARY
or
INTELLIGENCE SUMMARY

(Erase heading not required.)

Army Form C. 2118

Place	Date	Hour	Summary of Events and Information	Remarks and references to Appendices
CALONNE	July 8th		The day was spent in cleaning up and the C.O. & Officers went round the defences. A patrol of S.A.A. and Bombs Stores was got out and completed. The following were found on the night of the 8th.	
			31 OR. C. " for R.E. Tunnelling Co	
			26 " " B " " " "	
			70 " " B " for repairing line at DOUGHTY'S POST	
			13 " " D " VMG T.M.B	
			3 " " " " Do	
			52 " " D " R.E. Carriers	
			30 " " C " Brigade Bomb Store	
			50 " " D " R.E. Stores	
			30 " " E " Brigade Bomb Store	
"			The party under Captain Murphy, 2Lt Reyno & 2Lt Osborn amounting to 70 men were employed in repairing the line at DOUGHTY'S POST where our front line had been badly knocked about and to not tell. The enemy T.M's knocked the trench very much. Sergt Kirkby and 2 other ranks were killed and 7 were wounded. Also Capt. B.F. Murphy was slightly wounded. Private N. Munro "C" Co who was sentenced by F.G.C.M on 29th June, commuted to 10 years R.S. and entered suspended that himself through the foot when carrying sandbags, and was sent down	

WAR DIARY
or
INTELLIGENCE SUMMARY
(Erase heading not required.)

Army Form C. 2118

Place	Date	Hour	Summary of Events and Information	Remarks and references to Appendices
CALONNE	July 9th		**16 BUSHES.** W. In the early morning about 2am there was very heavy shelling on our left and a Gas Attack. Some of the attacking Battalion got gassed (reserve coy) sent up the S.O.S. signal. At 10.0pm someone on the right passed down the gas signal. Bells rang, and Horns Blown. We all donned our helmets but after about ½ hour it was cancelled. Some wind, and not a Gas Attack. We wondered how it could have come through satigues ? totalling 234 men. W.	
Do	July 10th		Quiet and humm day. About 3pm there was another false alarm of Gas owing to Brigade Operation, sending out Gas Alarm unless by Gas Alert. Orders came to relieve the 18th Potel tomorrow in the left sub sector. The 17th Potel being out place in support. At night we found 11 Fatigues amounting to 346 men. W.	
Do	July 11th		To-day we relieved the 18th Potel in the left sub sect (Avenne). The relief commenced at 3pm and was completed without incident at 6-30 p.m. During the night French Minn's Lie was directed from M.15.a. 9½.5. at Dieu it which is thought to hold a sniper. Before one generally very much more active than the last time we were in here. A machine gunner was hit by one. The Bullet entered his Helmet through & rear turn though's scalp and went out again slightly stunning him and scraping his scalp. The man has must previous taken the back and to "Stand a go at them" but has to be sent to	

1375 Wt. W593/826 1,000,000 4/15 J.B.C. & A. A.D.S.S./Forms/C. 2118.

Army Form C. 2118

WAR DIARY
or
INTELLIGENCE SUMMARY
(Erase heading not required.)

Instructions regarding War Diaries and Intelligence Summaries are contained in F.S. Regs., Part II. and the Staff Manual respectively. Title Pages will be prepared in manuscript.

Place	Date	Hour	Summary of Events and Information	Remarks and references to Appendices
CALONNE	July 12		The field ambulance. MB Between 12 & 12.30 am a charcoal fire was noticed in the enemy parapet. No wiring parties were out, nothing could be heard. One of our aeroplanes was flying over the lines and the enemy were very active with their search lights trying to pick it up. During the night, parties were working on in the trenches especially the front line trench on the left from Boyau 230 to Boyau 237 which has been as hotly knocked about by French mortars. This trench appears to have been knocked up apparently and now does not distort the life Company. There was a little T.M. fire on both sides but otherwise last night was very quiet. MB	
Do	July 13.		By patrol consisting of Corporal and 1 Green went out from Boyau 237 along the Killman but found nothing to report. Enemy snipers were very active during the night after a period of quietness. Generally a very quiet day. Fine & warm.	
Do	July 14		Sect No 2 was rather heavily shelled from 9am to noon. Trenches between Boyau 227 and 229 were heavily shelled by trench mortars but badly damaged - bombing was carried out in front of M. 15. C. 76. 30 rounds of Gayo fired with 9 Gooseberries, also 20	

1375 Wt W 393/826 1,000,000 4/15 J.B.C. & A. A.D.S.S./Forms/C. 2118.

WAR DIARY
or
INTELLIGENCE SUMMARY

Army Form C. 2118

(Erase heading not required.)

Place	Date	Hour	Summary of Events and Information	Remarks and references to Appendices
CALONNE	May 14th Cont		Parts of gap joined with trench line opposite Boyau 226 to 229. General repair of trenches was carried in all the front line, and on the Boyau. 2Lt Burroughs relieved from Tunnelling Coy and went in a curve to FOUQUIERES. 2Lt Prater relieved from the R.E. Coy and was attached to the Tunnelling Coy. Last night Patrols were sent out as follows. 1. 2Lt Enright & 2 N.C.O's. & 4 men went out from T.Head at M.15.c.43.3 at 11.05pm and returned at 1-15am but had nothing to report.	
CALONNE	May 16th		Last night Patrols as under went out. 1. Lt S. Haines and 2 men from Boyau 231, they found the German line opposite very regular and in good condition. 2. Cpt H.L. Leo & 4 men went out at M.15.C.23¾ at 11pm and found out line opposite poor and in bad condition. 3. Capt Murphy, Sergt Jones went out in front of Boyau 237 and found the mine on No 6 Coy front kept them and a lot of shell holes which would make good places for the enemy to congregate. 4. 2Lt Enright & a patrol went out at 11-30pm from T.Head M.15.c.4.3 and examined the German line, they found it in good condition. Enemy Wiring patrols were observed at the [illegible]. Very quiet and there appears to be	

WAR DIARY
or
INTELLIGENCE SUMMARY
(Erase heading not required.)

Army Form C. 2118

Place	Date	Hour	Summary of Events and Information	Remarks and references to Appendices
CALONNE	July 15th (Cont)		Nothing doing. Weather fine & warm.	
BULLY GRENAY	July 16th		Today we are relieved by the 18th Welch and go into Reserve at Bully GRENAY. The Relief commenced at 3pm without incident.	
	July 16th		The morning was devoted to resting the men and the afternoon to cleaning up. In the evening the café Chaplain Revd Williams held a voluntary Service in the Cinema. 50 men & 6 officers & 9 Sergts attended.	
Do	July 17th		Coys changed clothes at LES BREBIS and did some musketry. Weather Cooler.	
Do	July 18th		Lieut Thorn took over night OP occupied with the 119th Brigade Defence Scheme. Coys started from BULLY GRENAY at 11-30am and returned to BILLETS at 2-15am. Authority who received today to take 2/Lt O.P. TAYLOR, 2/Lt R.M. TAYLOR, 2/Lt H.K. JONES.	
			As our strength on attachment to French Trench Mortar Batteries — Reinforcements may now be demanded in their place — the officers with the Battalion now are as follows:-	

WAR DIARY or INTELLIGENCE SUMMARY

Army Form C. 2118

Place	Date	Hour	Summary of Events and Information	Remarks and references to Appendices
Bully GRENAY	July 1/2 (Con)		Attached to Head Quarters.	

Lt-Col. E.A. POPE. MAJOR C.B. HORE. CAPTAIN W.E. BROWN. LIEUT. J.K. SYMES.
2/Lt. F. ENRIGHT. 2/Lt. J.M. RENWICK. Lt. H.C. LLOYD. 2/Lt. J.E. REEVES.
"A" Coy.
CAPTAIN. WHITWORTH. CAPTAIN. J.W. FOREMAN. 2/Lt H.E.G. HOWELL.
"B" Coy.
CAPTAIN. MURPHY. Lt. J.S. LEWIS. 2/Lt A.G. OSBORN.
"C" Coy.
CAPTAIN. H.C. REES. CAPTAIN. C.M. PRITCHARD. 2/Lt J.V.B. WOOD. 2/Lt E.H. FRANCIS (sent to 'B' Coy.
(from next four days).
"D" Coy.
CAPTAIN. C.E. HOFFMEISTER. Lt. O.D. MORRIS. Lt. T.O. JONES. 2/Lt. H.J. BRUNN.
At LES BREBIS
Lt. Q.M. J. ALBUTT. TRANSPORT OFFICER Lt. R.J. DUCKHAM.
OFFICERS DETACHED
Lt. H.R. TAYLOR - Divisional Cuino Officer
Capt. A.G. AUSTEN. 1st Army School
2/Lt EDMONDS. Course M.G.
2/Lt. W. PROCTER Tunnelling Company. 16

Army Form C. 2118

WAR DIARY or INTELLIGENCE SUMMARY
(Erase heading not required.)

Place	Date	Hour	Summary of Events and Information	Remarks and references to Appendices
BULLY GRENAY	July 18th (con)		DEAD Lt A. NEWMAN. APPLYING FOR R.F.C. Lt D.R WILLIAMS M.O. ATTACHED. Lt A. VILES'D. R.A.M.C.	
Do.	July 19th		Today we relieved the 18th Welsh in the left sub section of CALONNE. The Relief was carried out without incident by 1pm. The night was a very quiet one, and usual work carried on.	
Do CALONNE	July 20th		Captain C.E. Hoffmeister inspected the wire in front of the Left Coy and found it weak in parts, Lt T.O'Jordo & 3 new men went out from Bogan 231 to within 10ft of the enemy wire. They met no working parties or patrols. The "Rifle Scheme" for this section was issued to Company Commanders today. Lt YORATH reports for duty and who goes to "A" Company.	
to CALONNE	July 21st		The weather was is fine though everything very quiet. in the evening Cpl. CM Pritchard with 3 N.C.O's and 12 men went out on a patrol, in the hopes of finding an enemy working party. Owing to a heavy artillery bombardment	

WAR DIARY
or
INTELLIGENCE SUMMARY
(Erase heading not required.)

Army Form C. 2118

Place	Date	Hour	Summary of Events and Information	Remarks and references to Appendices
CALONNE	July 21st (Cont)		on the left & a very bright moon they failed to find one. The patrol left at 10.35 p.m. & returned at 1.35 a.m. the following morning. Reports from Companies shew that considerable work has been carried on in the trenches.	
Do	July 22nd		The Battalion was relieved by the 11th Royal Scots the Relief started at 3.30 p.m. into LES BREBIS after the relief moved into LES BREBIS automatically open billets from the 14th H.L.I. Everything was ready for the Battalion on arrival in billets & tea was served at once to the men on arrival. The billets in LES BREBIS are very poor & consist of small houses most of which are decreasingly dirty.	
LES BREBIS	July 23rd		As today is Sunday there was Church Parade, 2 services were held in the Cinema, the afternoon was spent in cleaning up & resting.	
Do	July 24th		Whole day devoted to looking and cleaning, and there were Company Parades in the evening for inspection of arms clothing & Equipment.	

Army Form C. 2118

WAR DIARY
or
INTELLIGENCE SUMMARY
(Erase heading not required.)

Instructions regarding War Diaries and Intelligence Summaries are contained in F.S. Regs., Part II. and the Staff Manual respectively. Title Pages will be prepared in manuscript.

Place	Date	Hour	Summary of Events and Information	Remarks and references to Appendices
LES BREBIS	July 25th		The Adjutant, 2nd in Command, accompanied the C.O. on a reconnaissance of the GRENAY, BOUVIGNY line of trenches. The approaches to the LOOS and MAROC sections. The LENS Road Redoubts B.C.D. and E. in case we have to take up those positions in a defensive scheme. The whole Battalion furnish the Brigade working parties today & no men available for training. Musketry line thrown up.	
Do.	July 26th		Today the following officers arrived from Home and were posted to the Companies as under:- Lt. J.P. HARRISON 2Lt. W. POLLOCK } to "A" Coy. from 14th S.W.B. 2Lt. U.B. EDWARDS " H.B. PRICE } to "B" Coy. from 13th S.W.B. " W.J. WILLIAMS 2Lt. G. WELFORD " F.S. GREEN } to "C" Coy. from 14th S.W.B. 2Lt. M.H. WEBB " S. PRITCHARD } to "D" Coy. from 14th S.W.B.	

Army Form C. 2118

WAR DIARY
or
INTELLIGENCE SUMMARY
(Erase heading not required.)

Instructions regarding War Diaries and Intelligence Summaries are contained in F. S. Regs., Part II. and the Staff Manual respectively. Title Pages will be prepared in manuscript.

Place	Date	Hour	Summary of Events and Information	Remarks and references to Appendices
LES BREBIS	July 26th (Con)		Companies carried on Coy Training and Bombing. MB	
Do	July 27th		Weather fine & warm. Company training all day. MB	
Do	July 28th		Weather fine & warm. Company training all day. Aeroplanes dropped bombs in rear of these Billets close to where our men were drilling but did no damage. An R.E Officer & 4 men of the F.A. wounded by these MB Bombs.	
Do	July 29th		Last night some heavy shells were sent over into LES BREBIS. no damage was done to our Billets. MB Weather fine & warm. Coys carried on training and had a Staff Holiday in the afternoon as we are going up to the trenches tomorrow. MB	

1875 Wt. W593/826 1,000,000 4/15 J.B.C. & A. A.D.S.S./Forms/C. 2118.

Army Form C. 2118

WAR DIARY
or
INTELLIGENCE SUMMARY
(Erase heading not required.)

Instructions regarding War Diaries and Intelligence Summaries are contained in F. S. Regs., Part II. and the Staff Manual respectively. Title Pages will be prepared in manuscript.

Place	Date	Hour	Summary of Events and Information	Remarks and references to Appendices
LES BREBIS	July 30th		Today we relieved the 11th K.O.R.L's in THE CALONNE Subsection (We are left sub section). The relief started at 4 pm and was completed by 6.30pm without incident. The weather is very warm. Tonight is quiet with little activity on either side.	
CALONNE	July 31st		A very quiet day. Private Fowler while tinkering with an unexploded shell nearly blew one of his fingers off. The water has now been cut off at times for some days, and some inconvenience is felt tho' the weather is so warm. Our M.O. Lt D. VINEGIO has been indisposed for the last 3 days and Lt Williams R.A.M.C. is acting in his place. Lt J.P. Symes Assistant Adjutant has been attached to the 119th Brigade staff for duty. Our total strength all ranks today is 1054 including 38 officers of whom 8 are detailed for various purposes. Situation reports for today are "All quiet."	

Alexander Lt Col
Commanding 12 S.W.B.

119th Brigade.
40th Division.

12th BATTALION

SOUTH WALES BORDERERS

AUGUST 1916.

WAR DIARY
or
INTELLIGENCE SUMMARY

Army Form C. 2118

(12TH SERVICE BN., S.W.B. (3RD GWENT))

— AUGUST 1916 — VOL 3

3 X 19 sheets

Place	Date	Hour	Summary of Events and Information	Remarks and references to Appendices
CALONNE	Aug 1.		Last night a patrol consisting of Corporal Uthson & Corpl Hathaway, Private Oates & Private Meelings went out at M.G. d.21.2 at 10pm. Last night a Bosch sentry who seen & 10 Bombs were thrown into Enemy trench. Wiring Parties went out & a second patrol who sent out under 2/Lt Enright & 2/Lt Furbrook to investigated enemy sniper. W.O.	
DITTO	Aug 2.		T.M. Fire retaliated on their post Pine Trench. Snipers were rather busy & our Artillery & carried on work in trenches. All Companies Very Warm. W.O. Enemy shows greater activity both Snipers & T.M's Artillery than when we were there in June. Today the Artillery been very active. A patrol consisting of Corporal North, Pts Oates & Meeling went out to investigate the enemy wire. They reported that the enemy trenches opposite us appeared to be damaged. W.O. 2/-A.G. Ossian reported as acting were to day for duty as Assistant Adjutant.	
DITTO	Aug 3		Tonight and today considerable activity has been shewn by our Artillery. French Mortar & Machine Guns, and our own sent across numerous Rifle Grenades. The enemy has been busy with Whizz-bangs and small arms to pieces, particularly shelling Esoml	

Army Form C. 2118 — 2

WAR DIARY or INTELLIGENCE SUMMARY

Place	Date	Hour	Summary of Events and Information	Remarks and references to Appendices
CALONNE	Aug 3 (Cont)		Houses in DURHAM QUAD. German Snipers continue to be busy. A patrol went out for two hours last night and found three openings in the enemy's wire, also noticing that the grass was cut for about 6 yds in front of this wire. Evidently being done to prevent our patrols from obtaining cover near the wire. The weather continues fine & warm.	
DITTO	Aug 4		Sergt JONES T.M. men from 'B' Coy went out all night between 10pm & 2.15 am on a standing patrol to watch a gap in enemy's wire. They report a strong working party in rear of enemy front line trench at M.9.0.90. The fire of two Lewis guns was directed on them, and later the patrol reports that no further sounds were to be heard. O/C 'B' Coy (Capt B) had a demonstration at 3 am this morning, the occasion of the 21st Anniversary of the Coronation of the Ruler of the United States. Guns, Rifles, Trench Mortars, Rifle Grenades were brought into play, after three cheers for His Majesty had been given and Rule Britannia had been sung. The enemy retaliating with machine guns and 'whizz bangs' but did no damage in reparing their front.	(illeg)
DITTO	Aug 5		A patrol out last night reports that an enemy working party was engaged in repairing their front trench (illeg) in front of it.	(illeg)

WAR DIARY
or
INTELLIGENCE SUMMARY

(Erase heading not required.)

Army Form C. 2118

3

Place	Date	Hour	Summary of Events and Information	Remarks and references to Appendices
CAIX.NNE	AUG 5 (CON)		Some trench mortar guns fired upon the party at work. A huge explosion was observed in the enemy line on our left during a bombardment about 2am. The enemy has been very active of late with his light aerial torpedoes — "aerial darts". To our very deep regret Captain H.C. REES was killed by one of these this evening at about 7pm. Captain REES was an able and popular officer, much loved by his men, and his loss will be greatly felt by all of them. His death was a worthy one. The enemy was sending over a great many of the "aerial darts" and Captain REES was engaged in cheering his men and exhorting them to keep cool, when he was struck by one of the "darts" and killed instantaneously.	(iii)
DITTO	AUG 6		Last night Sergt. GRIMMETT and four men went out at 10pm for four hours on a patrol. They reported that after a French mortar shell had exploded in the enemy trench they distinctly heard a second explosion in the enemy line accompanied by screams. They consider that one shell blew up one of the German aerial guns.	(iii)
DITTO	AUG 7		A most unfortunate event occurred in the first river of this morning, involving the wounding of two officers and two other ranks, and the probable loss of one memo...	(iii)

WAR DIARY
or
INTELLIGENCE SUMMARY

Army Form C. 2118

Place	Date	Hour	Summary of Events and Information	Remarks and references to Appendices
CALONNE	Aug 7 (con)		A patrol went out to investigate some new work which had been observed in the enemy line. It was led by Captain W. Moorman, who took with him Lieut. E. R. Harvey (for instruction), Sergt Walter, & R. Fires Bert6, Cant & Pte Barnwell, 23rd. The party looked right Jup to the German wire and discovered itself a considerable party of Germans were there busy about. In order to find out the nature of the work Captain Moorman wished to observe the enemy longer and his party began to cut it. Some four client's had been cut when together Germans thought the patrol had been seen and gave the signal to challenge. Whereupon one of the party then threw a bomb, presumably at the German at front. Unfortunately this fell short, but the explosion roused some of the party who hurriedly killing the light, who rolls at present reported missing, Captain Moorman was severely wounded, Lieutenant Stouckel, T. Pl Snow slightly wounded, while Pte Barnwell is missing. No. The party made their way back to our wire as best they could; Captain Moorman arrived first. He was again wounded this way back by a bullet fm Machine Guns and Rifle fire were directed at the party immediately after Captain Moorman was helped	

WAR DIARY or INTELLIGENCE SUMMARY

Army Form C. 2118

Place	Date	Hour	Summary of Events and Information	Remarks and references to Appendices
CALONNE	AUG 7 (cont)		back from our line, and was at once seen to be seriously wounded. Shortly afterwards the 2/Lt. there arrived, the Stretcher himself assisted in both arms, had grown weak & Sgt. Harrison who was wounded, and had grown weak & collapsed. Twice made no mention of his own wounds, and never so the Stretcher did what he could to assist, only coming forward to have his own wounds (three) when the others that had been attended to.	
			Two parties subsequently went out to search for the missing men, but no trace of them could be found. (illd)	
DITTO	AUG 8		A further patrol went out last night to endeavour the search for the wounded, but they were unsuccessful in their quest. They located, however, a strongly working party of the enemy which was subsequently fired on by our Lewis Guns. (illd)	
DITTO	AUG 9		In the enemy trenches opposite the night there have been of late an almost complete absence of lamp lights. No patrolling was done by our men last night owing to the fact that our machine guns were firing to keep open the gaps in the enemy wire. (illd)	
DITTO	AUG 10		Last night the enemy searched for our trench mortar with MG's and H.E. Shells. Four of our men were wounded.	

WAR DIARY
or
INTELLIGENCE SUMMARY
(Erase heading not required.)

Army Form C. 2118

Place	Date	Hour	Summary of Events and Information	Remarks and references to Appendices
CALONNE	Aug 11.		A Patrol consisting of L/Cpls Coulson and Toon, Ptes Pickett and Matorys, went out at midnight, and made their way right up to the German wire opposite T bay. They made a careful investigation of it, and brought back the valuable information that the wire on the South side was only broken about 6ft. out, and that the wire on the North side was not cut at all. As they were coming back these parties of four were cut off but they successfully evaded them, and returned to T. head at 2.30 a.m. Aub.	
Ditto	Aug 12.		At 10.30 p.m. last night a Special Patrol went out to reconnoitre one more like gaps in the enemy's wire. The Patrol consisted of Captain Cecil Pritchard, 2/Lt Knight, 2/Lt 18 men. Scouts went first, the main patrol being immediately in rear, and the whole party got quite close to the German wire. They found that a strong enemy working party was repairing the back gate close to the main trench and that 3 Sentries patrolling up & down the gaps, and that the enemy was apparent no two quite on the alert. After letting his party lie for about two hours in	

WAR DIARY or INTELLIGENCE SUMMARY

Army Form C. 2118

Place	Date	Hour	Summary of Events and Information	Remarks and references to Appendices
CALONNE	Aug 12 (con)		...the off chance of capturing an enemy patrol. Captain Pritchard received that he was unable to reach observing further. In view of the operations which have been planned for tonight sensibly drew his party safely, and but the attention of the Trench Gunners ceased if the enemy party attempt interference at once fires on 1000.	
DITTO	Aug 13		The Battalion is congratulating itself today upon the accomplishment of a quite successful trip. The whole object of the trip was the capture of one or more strand of the purpose of discovering which enemy troops are now beyond the — a matter of great importance to the Higher Command, and this object was splendidly achieved by the capture of a sentry in the possession of an identity disc and his equipment. Unfortunately Captain S.W. Pritchard the leader of the raid, was severely wounded during the raid, and this somewhat mars the satisfaction in our eyes, but we cannot be other than greatly pleased to think that our Battalion was responsible for the first prisoner taken by the 40th Division. The enterprise had been planned with great care. Every detail was thoroughly considered, and everything	

Place	Date	Hour	Summary of Events and Information	Remarks and references to Appendices
CALONNE	Aug 13 (con)		engaged was made completely familiar with the part he had to play. The plans had the approval of the G.O.C. 1st Division and Colonel Buckley of the 40 Divisional Staff expressed the opinion that the scheme was the best that he had seen. The raiders were divided into four parties. Captain C.M. Kitchin in command of the raiders as a whole, took charge of the Centre Party; 2/Lt. F.L. Enright was in charge of the Right Party; and 2/Lt. Boys-Wood of the Left Party, whilst a Smaller Support Party was led by a N.C.O. The three attacking parties, each about a dozen strong, were made up of Bombers, Riflemen & Bomb Carriers. The Bombers wore bombing "breastcoats", carried a bucket of bombs apiece, and were further armed with clubs, the Riflemen also carried bomb buckets some of them taking two buckets of bombs in order to. (The Support Party carried the buckets in order that bombs each and had orders to go forth for more if necessary. At 10.30 p.m. the whole of three tongues left our T. Vlags Sap in single file. The left party, having made their long envelopy for the front the enemy's trench, each man making for the point allotted to him. The raiders were hardly in position	

WAR DIARY
or
INTELLIGENCE SUMMARY
(Erase heading not required.)

Army Form C. 2118

Instructions regarding War Diaries and Intelligence Summaries are contained in F. S. Regs., Part II. and the Staff Manual respectively. Title Pages will be prepared in manuscript.

Place	Date	Hour	Summary of Events and Information	Remarks and references to Appendices
LAVENTIE	Aug 13 (cont)		when the Artillery barrage that had been arranged for began. It had been timed to commence at midnight, and it was midnight to the second when the Artillery and machine Guns got to work in fine style. At once our attacking party moved forward and commenced operations on the enemy who however, immediately retaliated with rifle, machine Guns, and Shell fire. Captain Pritchard was almost at once wounded but he refused aid and jumped into the Huns trench, where he was successful in obtaining a prisoner. Meanwhile our Bombers were busy accounting for the enemy in the front line many of whom were killed. As soon as Artillery destroyer troops to the enemy any men to hinder retiring troops. Then already went from their own trenches to where to other men to our lines, and was obliged to hand them back to another Corps who brought the captured Bavarian over to Captain Pritchard himself was brought back by it. Swing the endeavour in a ready exhausted state. The whole of the Raiding Party were reported safe at 12.53am, and the Artillery through was ordered to cease. It was afterwards found, however,	

Army Form C. 2118

WAR DIARY
or
INTELLIGENCE SUMMARY
(Erase heading not required.)

10.

Place	Date	Hour	Summary of Events and Information	Remarks and references to Appendices
CARNOY	Aug 13 (Con)		that one man R. Thirteen - had not returned and he is still missing. Apart from this and the serious bombing of Captain Pritchard the affair had proved most satisfactory. Stretcher parties and M.O.'s Aid Post and all concerned behaved extremely well. All the wounded were brought back safely, many being carried in the open under fire. Or most the entire performance. The Artillery gave great assistance, both by enfilading the line with north their carefully-planned barrage & by their marine arrangement with (?) stokes mortars. Battalion M.O. worked extremely, the stretcher bearers worked speedily and efficiently dealt with and rapidly evacuated the Officers engaged behaved throughout with great gallantry, admirable judgement and keen enthusiasm and in accordance with the best traditions of the Army and set a fine example to their men who refused and enthusiastically followed it. The following Officers and N.C.O.'s. — private and (?) other men have been recommended for the Military Medal:— Lt. Col. E. Willan, L/Cpl. D'Ancaster, Pr. A.H. Skett, Pr. T. Bullen,	

Place	Date	Hour	Summary of Events and Information	Remarks and references to Appendices
CALONNE	Aug 13 (Cont)		Among the Raiders the following Casualties occurred:- 1 Officer (Capt. Pritchard) Severely wounded. 2 Other ranks Killed. 20 " " wounded (nine severely). In other peri- forming the following casualties occurred during the Raid, owing to retaliation:- 1 Officer (Captn Ct. Huffmaster) Dangerously wounded. 2 Other ranks Killed. 10 " " wounded. (aw)	
DITTO	Aug 13 (Cont)		The Battalion moved into Support at Calonne Village chg^y being relieved in the Front Line by the 18 Welsh Regt. (aw)	
DITTO	Aug 14		This morning we learnt to our great sorrow that Captain C.M. Pritchard had died of his wounds. The Battalion loses a very gallant officer and a churchman, grocer, and a large hearted gentleman. (aw)	

Place	Date	Hour	Summary of Events and Information	Remarks and references to Appendices
CALONNE	Aug 15		Yesterday the whole Battalion were on Fatigue duties (sic). In a communication from Divisional Headquarters received this morning it was announced that the late Captain C.M. Pritchard was to be recommended by the Major-General for Bravery & devotion to duty. It was further intimated that the Major-General has recommended Captain Pritchard to the D.S.O. but for the unfortunate death of the gallant officer. The Major-General expresses in such explicit terms that his recommendation be conveyed to the relatives of Captain Pritchard together with his regret at the loss of so gallant a Soldier. (sd)	
DO	Aug 16		The morning spent largely in cleaning up billets. The Battalion moved out to Caure at 2.30pm this afternoon taking our billets from the 1st R.I.F. We have to-day the Corps Commanders at Army Corps. No. 2406 Private R. Fox, No. 23324 Private A. Pickett, No. 23710 Private P. Bulten. authorised the military next to the following. the act of gallantry which gained them this distinction is described	

Army Form C. 2118

WAR DIARY
or
INTELLIGENCE SUMMARY
(Erase heading not required.)

Instructions regarding War Diaries and Intelligence Summaries are contained in F.S. Regs., Part II. and the Staff Manual respectively. Title Pages will be prepared in manuscript.

13.

Place	Date	Hour	Summary of Events and Information	Remarks and references to Appendices
CALONNE	Aug 16 (cont)		Under date August 14th. Private Pickett & Bullen took part in the raid of 12-13th. Pickett behaved splendidly all through. Unfortunately he is reported to have [?] Stretcher for bapts Butchard and wounds to bring him in. However he has fully recovered, the enemy mine or several nights before the raid, entered not valuable information. Private Bullen attempted to [?] many of the wounded in the open under fire, and was of the greatest assistance in bringing back the wounded Corp. Munro. Munro was wounded in the face, but continues to carry on his duties. (W.O)	
LES BREBIS	Aug 17		To-day was devoted mainly to bathing, resting, and cleaning up. Intimation was received this morning that L/Cpl Wilson, L/Cpl Laurents were both to be specially mentioned in Divisional Routine Orders for gallant conduct during the recent raid. (W.O)	
Do	Aug 18		The new Brigadier General (C. Cunliffe Owen) C.B. inspected the Battalion by Companies this morning, and expressed himself well pleased with the appearance and bearing of the men.	

WAR DIARY
or
INTELLIGENCE SUMMARY
(Erase heading not required.)

Army Form C. 2118

Place	Date	Hour	Summary of Events and Information	Remarks and references to Appendices
LES BREBIS	Aug. 19.		The whole Battalion being unengaged in R.E. fatigues.	
Do	Aug 20		Sunday. Church Parade was held in the morning. The C.O. Lt. Col. Hon. L.C.W. Palk in command went to Church at BRAQUEMONT, afterwards the service the Brigadier Commander Brigadier General Walker visited the Herals & congratulated men who had received mention in recent orders. Sgt. A. Parker, L/C Bollen, Recevies, the military medal. Private R. Jones was in hospital and could not be present. Pride Compton Wickens was congratulated in receiving mention in O.T.O., Private Lancaster was in hospital so could not be present. The Coy. Commander made a short speech conveying the work of the No. Division in the short time it has been out. Weather fine & warm.	
Do	Aug 21.		Companies carried out Company training all day and Nos Companies went on a short Route march in the evening.	
Do	Aug 22		Company training all day, route marches in the evening	

WAR DIARY or INTELLIGENCE SUMMARY

Army Form C. 2118

Place	Date	Hour	Summary of Events and Information	Remarks and references to Appendices
LES BRÉBIS	Aug 22 (Con)		At 10-45 pm a heavy bombardment by our guns started & lasted until 12-15. It is understood that the 11th K.R.R. were carrying out a minor operation. Information was received at 12 midnight that the 119th Brigade were relieving the 117th Brigade in the hour section on the 24/25th inst. We had made arrangements to relieve the A & C.H. in Caltoma left tomorrow, but this will now be cancelled. 2nd Froncs relieved the Buckhum relieving to go to Hospital as Transport Officer for the Battn to-day. The C.O. received the following letter from Colonel E.S. Heathcote late Brigadier-General of this Brigade. It speaks for itself. "Time does not allow me of my Goodbye and to thank you for all the Goodwork you have done while we have served together. You can be justly proud of your Section, and I if it entitled to inform you it undoubtedly has saved the strain of the trenches, shall look forward for great things." My best wishes, your Division was the finest	

WAR DIARY
or
INTELLIGENCE SUMMARY

Army Form C. 2118

Place	Date	Hour	Summary of Events and Information	Remarks and references to Appendices
LES BREBIS	Aug 22 (cont)		at Divisional Headquarters, which was the headquarters I have seen since I joined the Division. Yours Sincerely C. F. Pritchard Lt Col	
Do	Aug 23		The whole Battalion today was engaged in R.E. fatigues and in cleaning up billets etc.	
Do LOOS	Aug 24		The Battalion moved out from the billets at Les Brebis this morning, and relieved the 18th R. Munster Fusiliers in the left Subsection of the Loos Sector. The relief was taken over by the 19th R. Welsh Fusiliers. Information has been received today that the G.O.C. Commanding-in-Chief has awarded the Military Cross to 2/Lt J. P. Wood, for cool & courageous conduct on the night of the Raid (12/13 August) when Captain Pritchard was a wounded. Wood went & took charge of the German prisoners and conducted them back to our trenches. After handing him over, & although running heavily from a Rifle bullet wound of the arm, he again went back to the starting trench. It was this cool conduct	

WAR DIARY or INTELLIGENCE SUMMARY

Army Form C. 2118

Place	Date	Hour	Summary of Events and Information	Remarks and references to Appendices
Loos	Aug 24 (cont)		materially worsened the life below the ridges. WW	
Do	Aug 25		The enemy were very quiet last night. They did no patrols out and offered no interference to our wiring operations. Very few Very lights were sent up from the German front, but no sounds of activity were heard. WW	
Do	Aug 26		Our trench mortar dispersed an enemy working party which was observed last night between Gordon & Seaforth Alleys. Observation is difficult from our trenches owing to the contour. Our artillery officers is endeavouring to find a suitable position for an Observation Post. WW	
Do	Aug 27		Last night L/Sgt Burton and 3 men patrolled the craters in front of Boyau 44, and reported being worked on right and left of centre. The wire in front of our own trench is in a very bad state, and all companies in the front line have been at work upon it. WW	

WAR DIARY
or
INTELLIGENCE SUMMARY
(Erase heading not required.)

Army Form C. 2118

18.

Place	Date	Hour	Summary of Events and Information	Remarks and references to Appendices
LOOS	Aug 28		Everything was quiet last night on our front. A Stray shot however killed Sgt- Waters who was out with a wiring party. The Battalion was relieved today by the 1st Welsh Regt. and moves into Reserve at Mons March taking over billets from the 12th Suffolks. NW	
MAROC	Aug 29		Today was devoted to cleaning up, and bathing at the Divisional Baths at La Brebis. The following officers joined the Battalion this morning, and were posted to Companies as under.— Captain J.C.B. Taggett } to 'A' Company Lieut. E.A. Shelfoe } Captain G.O. Tyte } to 'B' Company Lieut. J.D. Greaves } Lieut. J.S. Urquart } to 'C' Company Lieut. J.A. Hill } to 'D' Company. NW	
DITTO	Aug 30		The Battalion carried on work today in the improvement of Billets. The weather was more or less stormy, and many of the cellars were temporarily flooded. Two more Officers reported for duty with the Battalion	

Place	Date	Hour	Summary of Events and Information	Remarks and references to Appendices
MAROC	Aug 30 (cont)		This afternoon – 2/Lt A.W. Mackay posted to 'B' Coy and 2/Lt G.L. Jones posted to 'C' Coy.	
MAROC	Aug 31.		Improvement of Billets was carried on again today. Especially with a view to prevent flooding in future.	

Alexander Lieut. Colonel.
Comdg. 12th Bn. South Wales Borderers.

119th Brigade.
40th Division.

12th BATTALION

SOUTH WALES BORDERERS

SEPTEMBER 1916.

WAR DIARY or INTELLIGENCE SUMMARY

Army Form C. 2118.

12 S.W.B
SEPTEMBER 1916

Place	Date	Hour	Summary of Events and Information	Remarks and references to Appendices
LOOS	1/9		The Battalion relieved the 18th Welsh Regt in the Left Sector, LOOS, Today, the Welsh moving into the Billets at NORTH MAROC. A patrol consisting of Lts J.C. Lewis and Enright, 2/Lt Urquart and Sgt Picket went out at 10.30pm tonight to investigate the state of the Enemy wire out side of our line against the canal. They minutely discovered a strong bosche working party in front, between a strong wire entanglement to dispose of which were well in front of this wire. The Enemy had laid a bomb setting, about 5ft high. in covering their front.	
"	2/9		Last night two extraordinarily quiet. The Enemy sent up very few very lights, and hardly fired a Shot. At 8.10pm today the Enemy exploded a mine, and at once Captain B.G. Murphy ordered 2/Lts Lewis + 2/Lt N.C. Urquart to take a party of men to SEAFORTH CRATER. They did So and entered + bombed the Enemy's sap. A report came to Bn Headquarters that the Enemy had penetrated our front line and artillery support was asked for. GHQ reports subsequently	
"	3/9			

Army Form C. 2118.

WAR DIARY
or
INTELLIGENCE SUMMARY
(Erase heading not required.)

Place	Date	Hour	Summary of Events and Information	Remarks and references to Appendices
LOOS	4/9		proved to be without foundation. The enemy put up a strong Barrage on our support & Reserve lines, and did considerable damage to the trenches.	
"	5/9		At tonight afterwards took a patrol to the Enemy line. They entered the Enemy front line trench and examined the New Crater, but found it to be deserted. A Party of five men were unfortunately gassed by fumes from a Mine Shaft, and two of them died from effects.	
"	6/9		All was quiet on our front today. Our own men were busily engaged in work in the trenches and in wiring. Today & two has been very quiet again on the whole of our front. Very great improvements have been made in the trenches by our men, and a considerable amount of wiring have been done.
The Battalion was relieved today by the 18th Welsh Regt and moved into support, the dispositions being as follows:-	

Army Form C. 2118.

WAR DIARY
or
INTELLIGENCE SUMMARY
(Erase heading not required.)

Place	Date	Hour	Summary of Events and Information	Remarks and references to Appendices
LOOS	7/9		"A" Coy. } In the Enclosure, Loos. "B" Coy. } "C" Coy. less 1 Platoon, in Duke St. "C" Coy. 1 Platoon in Wellington Keep, Loos Redoubt. "D" Coy. 2 Platoons in Village Line "D" Coy. 2 Platoons in Loos Rd. Redoubt. Headquarters and Headqrs Company at Ponte Passage.	
"	8/9		The whole Battalion, with the exception of the Platoons in Loos Rd Redoubt and Wellington Keep, was engaged on fatigue for the R.E.s and scavenging Coy. C. the platoons in the Redoubt & keep form the Garrison of those places, and must not turn out. They worked in improving their quarters.	
"	9/9		Fatigue again. The Bn has been "on fatigue" as yesterday. Considerable improvements have been made at Headquarters. Similar fatigues occupied the Bn again today. Major Bethune took over temporary Command of the 1/Welsh Rgt. today, during the absence on leave of Col Wilkie.	

Army Form C. 2118.

WAR DIARY
or
INTELLIGENCE SUMMARY
(Erase heading not required.)

Place	Date	Hour	Summary of Events and Information	Remarks and references to Appendices
LOOS	10/9		The whole Bn was today engaged in fatigues, or in improving the trenches we occupy.	
LES BREBIS	11/9		The Battalion was relieved today by the 13 Yorks Regt and moved into Billets in (Sc Pe) Brebis, taking over the Billets from the same Regt.	
"	12/9		The cleaning of clothes, rifles & equipment was occupied the Bn today.	
"	13/9		The whole Bn was engaged today in R.E. fatigues.	
"	14/9		The morning was devoted to further cleaning up. This afternoon the C.O. inspected the Bn by Companies, and expressed himself well satisfied at their general appearance.	
"	15/9		The Bn carried on training today from 9.0 am until 12 noon & from 5:30pm to 7.30pm. Two Companies went on a route march.	
"	16/9		This morning was devoted to training, the afternoon being left free as a "half holiday".	
"	17/9		The whole Bn was on R.E. fatigue again today. The weather continues to be fine.	

WAR DIARY or INTELLIGENCE SUMMARY

Army Form C. 2118.

Place	Date	Hour	Summary of Events and Information	Remarks and references to Appendices
LES BREBIS	18/9		Battalion carried on training, trained most of the day. C.O. & Coy. Officers reconnoitred MAROC & position	
MAROC LEFT	19/9		We relieved the 11th Kings Own (Lancashire) in MAROC left Sub Section. Relief commenced with guides at 4pm and was completed by 5.30pm without incident. The bowl at 3pm was quiet. The enemy sentries after 7pm in the Double Crassier, that did no damage. The rain of the last few days have made the trenches very bad and a lot of clearing has to be done. Rain all day. Twenty. fairly quiet till the evening. In the line this Coy are distributed as follows:- Front line Right 'A' Co Front line Left 'D' Co Support line Right 'B' Co Support line Left 'C' Co which is held by both Coys. We have a Special Section of 6 Bombers who holds it. The Germans also have Bombers & the line in places are only a few yards away and a great alertness has to be maintained.	
"	20/9			

Place	Date	Hour	Summary of Events and Information	Remarks and references to Appendices
MARET (LEFT)			Owing to the fact that the German Division opposite us has not been identified we are ordered to undertake a minor operation for the purpose of obtaining identification & prisoners. This is going to be an unusually business, as the wire here is very thick in places, entrances, and very strong. 2/Lt Wingart conducted a small raiding party to the enemy sap at apex of "Triangle". The 4 men occupying the sap were bombed but could not be caught. The party entered the sap and brought away two boxes of bombs. Capt. G.D.Page conducted another party on a reconnaissance and discovered an enemy working party in strength. They were ordered before going out not to enter into any engagement so withdrew. About 9 o'clock this evening the enemy carried out an intense T.M. Bombardment in the Southern Gassis and we had several casualties - 3 deaths.	
"	29/9		Rain all day. Enemy very quiet. 2/Lt Wingart & Capt. G.D.Page conducted a patrol to examine enemy wire. Snipers were active during the day.	

Army Form C. 2118.

WAR DIARY
or
INTELLIGENCE SUMMARY

(Erase heading not required.)

Place	Date	Hour	Summary of Events and Information	Remarks and references to Appendices
MAROC.	22/9.		Severe retaliation in the Southern Crassier, retaliation was asked for, but is very tardy.	
"	23/9		Enemy T.M's here again very active in the Southern Crassier causing many casualties. Enemy Artillery searched our Support line presumably for T.M.'s lately they have been very chary of using Artillery. The C.O. went down to Berlougal for a C.O's Conference at 1st Army School CANDATTE. and meanwhile 2nd in Command of the Battalion 2/Lt. Clongard & 2/Lt. St. Brown hunted a patrol at Barriere Steps with Sgt. Pickett & Farmer and 7 O.R. to cover the ground for a proposed Raid tomorrow night. Minor Operations have carried out by the B.C.C. on our left. The midseat- gotten officer with good identification.	
"	24/9		A quiet day until Evening - at 9.15 the 17 Welsh attempted a minor Operation. It was preceded by intense Artillery bombardment on a Bavarian trench kept up. They took one man(?) missing & did not obtain identification.	

WAR DIARY or INTELLIGENCE SUMMARY

Army Form C. 2118.

Place	Date	Hour	Summary of Events and Information	Remarks and references to Appendices
MAROC (LEFT)			At 12.30am 2/Lt Toingard & 2/Lt Brown Sgt. Tanner picked & Nelson 30 o.ranks attempted a Raid on the Enemy trench. Previous to the Raid an Alarm of Gas was passed on from the Brigade on right in error, which bothered the proceedings from 11.30pm to 12.30am. The party got into the Enemy front line - to the parapet. 2/Lt Toingard & Sgt Tanner picked & 2 o.ranks got into the enemy trench 2/Lt Toingard shot 2 Germans but was blown up onto the parapet by a small Can mine. Shot in the trench shortly wounded. Seeing the volume of smoke gone the Alarm of Gas returned. Sgt picked Tanner were stunned by the explosion. Sgt Tanner bombed Enemy dugouts in the Enemy trench. Owing to the fact that shot in the trench were stunned by the explosion no identification were obtained. Lt Toingard was carried back but unfortunately died of wounds early in the morning of the next day on his way to the Hospital.	8
	26/9			

Place	Date	Hour	Summary of Events and Information	Remarks and references to Appendices
MAPLE (LEFT)	26/9		Our Casualties were:- 1 Officer killed 1 O.R. killed 10 O.R. slightly wounded (mostly at duty). Lonegan is a great loss to the Battalion. He was a Canadian and served as the trenches with the 7th Battalion, having been mentioned in despatches for raiding work. He was so extraordinarily fearless even, always keen to attempt anything with danger in it. Everyone liked him; he was noted for rapid promotion, and we have no one else in the Battalion who was quite so much dead on the job. The two buried at NOEUX-LES-MINES Cemetery on the 26th. Lt. R. Symes H. Albert attended the funeral.	
	27/9		A quiet day after the raid. Orders were issued for the relief tomorrow by the Rhodesh. We sent some more into support of relieve the 19th RW Fusiliers, who go in on the Right.	

Army Form C. 2118.

WAR DIARY
or
INTELLIGENCE SUMMARY
(Erase heading not required.)

Place	Date	Hour	Summary of Events and Information	Remarks and references to Appendices
MAROC	28/9		Special vigilant was maintained in the line last night, no warning of a supposed German concentration opposite no was received at Headquarters. The Battalion was relieved today by the 18th Welsh Regt and moved into Support in N.E. of BRCE, taking over Billets from the 19th Rws Fusiliers	
"	29/9		The whole Battalion was today engaged in fatigues in cleaning up. The Commanding Officer (Major Bryan in the absence of Colonel Pope) inspected the Billets this afternoon.	
"	30/9		The Battalion was still engaged in Fatigue Party.	

J B Hope Major
Lieut. Colonel.
Comdg. 12th Bn. South Wales Borderers.

119th Brigade.
40th Division.

12th SOUTH WALES BORDERERS

OCTOBER 1916.

Army Form C. 2118

40/12 RSWB?
Vol 5

5 x 6 sheets

WAR DIARY
or
INTELLIGENCE SUMMARY
(Erase heading not required.)

Instructions regarding War Diaries and Intelligence Summaries are contained in F.S. Regs., Part II. and the Staff Manual respectively. Title Pages will be prepared in manuscript.

Place	Date	Hour	Summary of Events and Information	Remarks and references to Appendices
MAROC	Oct 1st		The Battalion moved from support to Reserve today, interchanging billets with the 17th Welsh Regt.	
	2nd		The men were largely on fatigues today the C.O. (Maj. E.B. Hone) inspected the billets which were generally good, most of the men had been, and the billets are usually dry, comfortably well ventilated) The Bn. M.O. Lieut S Williams left the Bn today, his place has been taken by Lieut H.L. McCormick R.A.M.C.	
	3rd		Fatigues again occupied most of Bn today.	
	4th		Major C.B. Hone left the Bn today, to our great regret, to take command of 10th R.W.F. In the absence of Col. E.B. Soltis on leave, Major D.F. Murphy assumed command of Bn.	
	5th		Bn moved into front line today, taking over left sub sector MAROC from 18th 13th Welsh Regt. The 19th R.W. moved into the billets vacated by us. Our dispositions in the line are as follows:— Left Front "B" Co Right Front "A" Co Support "C" Co Support "D" Co	
	6th		The enemy is very quiet, no working parties have been heard. Our trenches are in a very bad state. The following is an extract from "London Gazette" dated 4th Oct 1916.	

1875 Wt. W593/326 1,000,000 4/15 J.B.C. & A. A.D.S.S./Forms/C. 2118.

WAR DIARY
or
INTELLIGENCE SUMMARY

(Erase heading not required.)

Army Form C. 2118

Instructions regarding War Diaries and Intelligence Summaries are contained in F. S. Regs., Part II. and the Staff Manual respectively. Title Pages will be prepared in manuscript.

Place	Date	Hour	Summary of Events and Information	Remarks and references to Appendices
	Oct 6th		The undermentioned Temporary Captains to be "Temporary Majors":— H.C. Rees (wounded in action) 7th July B.F. Murphy 6th Aug. The undermentioned Temporary Lieutenants to be Temp. Captains:— R.A. Kerman — Ansden 20th Mar O.S. Morris 7th July H.C. Lloyd 6th Aug J.O. Jones 15th Aug The undermentioned Temp'y 2nd Lieuts to be Temp'y Lieutenants:— J.E. Reeves 7th July A.J. Osborn 6th Aug J.B. — ev Ord 15th Aug	
	7th		The enemy's T.M's were constantly firing through today. Our Stokes T.M's retaliated & sent over many rifle grenades especially on the right & its Grazies. Our Aerial was night reported an the enemy working party which was observed by own M.G. fire	
	8th		A Trench Mortar in Lerrzyn St was blown up early this morning — Lemun & his 2 comrades belonged between Griever to xthe front line. A larger being formed 2nd along by 2nd deep.	

1875 Wt. W593/826 1,000,000 4/15 J.B.C. & A. A.D.S.S./Forms/C. 2118.

WAR DIARY or INTELLIGENCE SUMMARY

Army Form C. 2118

(Erase heading not required.)

Place	Date	Hour	Summary of Events and Information	Remarks and references to Appendices
Maroc	Oct 8th		Last night all was quiet. Bright moonlight prevented any work, except on the right, where an examination of the wire was made.	
"	9th		We had two patrols out last night, one investigated the enemy's sap head, & discovered at M.6.5.4.2, & found the enemy's sap unoccupied. The presence of two crossbands & small wire barricade gave the appearance that it is possibly used as a listening post. The other reconnoitred the enemy wire opposite M.5. to M.55. & found the wire cut in places by our artillery, & encountered a strong enemy wiring party.	
"	10th		A strong patrol under 2 Lts. Lennie went out at 1.30 am from Sap 6 (M.4.d.6.9) (2nd Lt Greene) sereved several enemy working parties & our M.G. fire was directed on them. An enemy patrol among our defences our left company approaches but a special patrol sent out.	
"	11th		A fighting patrol under Lieut L.L. Lennie went out at 9.30 pm. They established themselves as the heads of the HUN sap, they tried to cut some wire but were discovered by the enemy who attacked them with bombs & rifle fire. Fortunately most of the bombs were duds & our patrol retaliated with bombs. The enemy of unknown numbers then retired. Very thick in this part of the line.	

WAR DIARY or INTELLIGENCE SUMMARY

Army Form C. 2118

(Erase heading not required.)

Instructions regarding War Diaries and Intelligence Summaries are contained in F.S. Regs., Part II. and the Staff Manual respectively. Title Pages will be prepared in manuscript.

Place	Date	Hour	Summary of Events and Information	Remarks and references to Appendices
Mars	12/10/16		The Battalion was relieved by the 18th Welch Regt & moved into support. The relief was completed without incident.	
	13/10/16		A. Col. Sone returned from leave. The O. rank & section of chort in reserve & 45 junior Reps. have been enquiring.	
	14/10/16		The M.O. Lieut M Cormick left the Bn 10 days ambulance by new Orders. This officer only stayed the day & was relieved on the 15th by Capt. G.O. Rethdon R.A.M.C. like the who had been on the 13th but there has been no indents in rest on fatigues.	
	15/10/16 16/10/16		The Bn moved into reserve in M+ROC, taking over from 15th Welch Regt.	
	17/10/16		The Bn were engaged on fatigues. Billets were indifferent by the Corps Commander General Anderson. The front line has been reported as being combed with heavy T.M.s today a case of growse was brought in where M.O. has taken the necessary steps.	
	18/10/16 19/10/16		The whole Bn was engaged in various fatigues & when off duty making up efficiencies in equipment, cleaning up. The M.O. enquired M.O. On every of the trenches & health was very good, but men were shewing signs of fatigue.	

1875 Wt. W593/826 1,000,000 4/15 J.B.C. & A. A.D.S.S./Forms/C. 2118.

Army Form C. 2118

WAR DIARY
or
INTELLIGENCE SUMMARY
(Erase heading not required.)

Instructions regarding War Diaries and Intelligence Summaries are contained in F. S. Regs., Part II. and the Staff Manual respectively. Title Pages will be prepared in manuscript.

Place	Date	Hour	Summary of Events and Information	Remarks and references to Appendices
MAROC. LOOS.	20.10.16.		The Battalion was moved today from the Reserve to Front line, taking over the Left Sub Section, of the (new) LOOS SECTOR from the 19th R.W.F. who replaced us in the Billets in MAROC. The Adjutant (Capt. W.E.Brown) left to go on leave today. His place is taken by Lieut. J.R.Symes and Lieut.A.G.OSBORN reported to Battn.H.Q. as Assistant Adjutant. The Battalion is disposed in the line as follows :- "B" Coy, "A" Coy, Right Front Line; "C" & "D" Coys Support (In Enclosure).	
"	21.10.16.		Last night was very quiet and today has been quiet too, except for intermittent activity of an enemy Trench Mortar, which fires upon one sector of our line. Lieut. J.E.Reeves and 2/Lt. W.J.E.Proctor received orders this evening to proceed to England on a Machine Gun Course. They left the Battalion during the course of the evening.	
LOOS.	22.10.16.		The night was quiet except for enemy's M.G.Fire, but part of our line (M.6.1. and 2) is liable at any moment to Trench Mortars and Aerial Darts activity. There rarely fire at night, however.	
"	23.10.16.		The enemy's Machine Guns were extremely active during the whole of last night. One or two enemy working parties were located by our covering parties (for our wiring parties). The enemy's Trench Mortars have not been so active today. At dusk, however, his M.G.Guns are very busy. The C.O. (Lieut-Colonel.E.A.Pope) went tonight to Brigade Headquarters to act as Brigadier General in the absence of General Cunliffe Owen (on duty at Divisional Headquarters). The C.O. will however, come up to the Battalion each dya for a few hours.	
"	24.10.16.		Last night Lieut.J.S.Lewis and two O.R. went out to investigate the enemy's wire and. sap at about M.6.B.2.O. and gained information which will be of use in the forthcoming raid. The Comapnies changed over in the lines today, "A" & "B" moving into Support in the Enclosure, and "C" & "D" Coy replacing them in the Front Line — "C" on the Right, "D" on the Left.	
"	25.10.16.		Last night was fairly quiet, enemy's T.M.'s sent over a few "rum jars" during the night. During the night the enemy was observed to throw a few bombs into his own wire between HARRISONS Crater & MANNINGS Mound. Lieut.Lewis and 4 O.R.went out on patrol and found the enemy engaged in repairing the gaps in his wire about M.6.D.20.95. Lewis Guns were directed on to the party at work, and fired at frequent intervals throughout the night. Three other patrols went out, but found nothing to report.	

Army Form C. 2118

WAR DIARY
or
INTELLIGENCE SUMMARY

(Erase heading not required.)

Instructions regarding War Diaries and Intelligence Summaries are contained in F.S. Regs., Part II. and the Staff Manual respectively. Title Pages will be prepared in manuscript.

Place	Date	Hour	Summary of Events and Information	Remarks and references to Appendices
LOOS.	25.10.16	(Contd)	The enemy seems to be more active than usual. Throughout today he has been intermittently shelling - chiefly in or near the Enclosure, where he did damage and inflicted casualties.	
"	26.10.16.		Two Patrols were out last night. One under 2/Lieut.Pollock found enemy alert in trenches at about M.6 .D.30.95 apparently watching closely the gap in his wire. The other out opposite DEAD MAN'S SAP found the enemy wire very thick here, nut saw no sign of the enemy. The Enclosure seems to be under close observation. On two occasions smoke from a fire drew instant fire from the enemy, which ceased immediately the smoke was got under.	
"	27.10.16.		Four of our patrols were out last night. All of them found the enemy busily at work at points in his trenches. Little sniping was observed last night from the enemy. Our Machine Guns opened directly upon the enemy working parties and was maintained at intervals throughout the night.	
"	28.10.16.		The raid arranged for last night had at the last minute to be abandoned owing to a mis-understanding. The party detailed to lay/the Bangalore were however unable to carry out their task, and found the enemy wire alertly watching the gap through which the raid was to take place. Consequently it appears that even if the raid had been proceeded with as arranged, it would have been difficulty to accomplish. Trench Mortar activity continues on both sides, otherwise things are quiet now.	
"	29.10.16.		Trench Mortar activity still continues on both sides. Our artillery.retaliated effectively. The Battalion today moved to LES BREBIS being relived by the 9th Bn.Royal Sussex Regt.	
LES BREBIS.	30.10.16		The Battalion were today occupied in fitting gas helmets & testing, bathing & replacing deficiencies. The C.O. inspected the Battalion by Companies.	
"	31.10.16.		The Battalion moved out of LES BREBIS at 9.13.a.m. today en route for BRUAY	

Lieut. Colonel,
Cmdg. 12th Bn. South Wales Borderers.

119th Brigade.
40th Division.

12th BATTALION

SOUTH WALES BORDERERS

NOVEMBER 1916.

Notes Confidential
Volume 1

12 SWB Vol 6

Army Form C. 2118.

WAR DIARY
or
INTELLIGENCE SUMMARY.
(Erase heading not required.)

Instructions regarding War Diaries and Intelligence Summaries are contained in F. S. Regs., Part II. and the Staff Manual respectively. Title pages will be prepared in manuscript.

Place	Date	Hour	Summary of Events and Information	Remarks and references to Appendices
BRUAY.	Nov. 1st.		Continuing their march, the 119th Brigade group left BRUAY today, the Battalion being alloted the billeting Area "A" MONCHY BRETON. Headed by "B" Coy they left at 9-20.a.m. arriving about 1.30.p.m. The men again marched well and on arrival were billeted in barns and hay lofts. After dinners had been served, the men had feet inspection and the remainder of the day was devoted to cleaning rifles and equipment.	
MONCHY BRETON.	Nov. 2nd		The 119th Brigade Group, today continued their march, AREA "E". MONTS-EN-TERNAS being alloted to the Battalion. Leaving at 8-30.a.m. they arrived at their destination about 12.15.p.m. It was a very wet day and the roads were in a very bad state, but after the men had been served with dinner, the weather cleared considerably, and after foot inspection, the men were given arms drill and instruction in the use of the New Small Gas Box Respirator.	
MONTS-EN-TERNAS.	Nov. 3rd		Today was again devoted to drill, bayonet fighting and lectures, and instruction in the use of the Small Box Gas Respirator. The weather was showery.	
"	Nov. 4th		In accordance with 119th Infantry Brigade Orders, The Battalion marched from AREA "E" to AREA "H" BONNIERES, today, leaving at 8-20.a.m. they arrived at noon.	
BONNIERES.	Nov. 5th		They were billeted in barns and hay lofts and after the usual foot inspections, the remainder of the day was devoted to cleaning rifles and equipment.	
"	"		Starting at 10-0.a.m. the Battalion marched to AUTHEUX arriving there at 1-0'clock. The Billets were rather crowded owing to the 119th Brigade being also billeting in the Area. It was a fine day, but the stiff wind and the hills made marching rather heavy.	
AUTHEUX.	Nov. 6th.		Coy Training was carried out all day. Owing to showers this had to be curtailed considerably. About 10 to 10-30 an intense red glow was noticed in the sky to the East. No one knows what it was. Possibly an ammunition dump blown up. It lasted for about an half hour.	
"	Nov. 7th.		Very heavy rain all day., stopped all training. Some men of "A" Coy raided a wine cellars and are alleged to have taken 52 bottles. The case was investigated by the C.O. and reported to Brigade.	
"	Nov. 8th		The weather improved slightly today, and all Companies carried on training.	

Army Form C. 2118.

WAR DIARY
or
INTELLIGENCE SUMMARY.
(Erase heading not required.)

Instructions regarding War Diaries and Intelligence Summaries are contained in F.S. Regs., Part II. and the Staff Manual respectively. Title pages will be prepared in manuscript.

Place	Date	Hour	Summary of Events and Information	Remarks and references to Appendices
AUTHEUX	Nov.8th		By order of the Brigadier General the whole of "A" Coy vacated their billets and moved to MON PLAISIR FARM. The C.O. lectured all Officers this evening on the ATTACK - TRENCH TO TRENCH.	
"	Nov.9th.		All Companies continued training today, the weather being very fine. The following inter-change of Officers took place today :- Capt.E.E.A.Whitworth Posted to "B" Coy. " T.O.Jones " " "A" " " H.C.Lloyd " " "D" " The C.O. gave another useful lecture to Officers.	
"	Nov.10th		The Companies practised the Attack "TRENCH TO TRENCH" today, and did very well. The C.O. continued his lectures to Officers on the "ATTACK", dealing tonight with the consolidation of a captured trench.	
"	Nov.11th.		Captain.E.E.A.Whitworth was re-posted to "A" Coy today, Capt.T.O.Jones remaining with "A" as 2nd in-Command, and Lieut.J.S.Lewis was posted to "B" Coy, vice Capt.H.C.Lloyd who returns to "B" Coy. All Companies carried out training as usual. and the C.O.concluded his lectures to Officers on the "ATTACK".	
"	Nov.12th		Today being Sunday, we had a Church Parade in the morning, while in the afternoon the C.O. conducted an hour's Battalion Training.	
"	Nov.13th		Company Drill was carried out all day, also Battalion Drill by the C.O..	
"	Nov.14th		Company & Battalion Training all day. Orders were received late at night for a move to FORTEL. This is back in our tracks and only a mile from BONNIERES	
"	Nov.15th.		The Battalion paraded at 11-0.a.m. and marched to FORTEL. There was a very cold wind, but the day improved. Arrived at FORTEL at 3.0.p.m. Men's billets rather cramped, Officers Billets quite good.	
FORTEL.	Nov.16th.		At FORTEL the Battalion carried out Battalion Training and Company Work. The C.O.went to Brigade to act as temporary Brigader, and Major.B.F.Murphy took over command pth of the	

Army Form C. 2118.

WAR DIARY
or
INTELLIGENCE SUMMARY.
(Erase heading not required.)

Instructions regarding War Diaries and Intelligence Summaries are contained in F. S. Regs. Part II. and the Staff Manual respectively. Title pages will be prepared in manuscript.

Place	Date	Hour	Summary of Events and Information	Remarks and references to Appendices
FORTEL.	Nov. 16th	(cpntd)	Battalion temporarily. Advice was received late to proceed to BONNIERES.	
FORTEL.	Nov. 17th		The Battalion paraded at 10-0.a.m. and marched to BONNIERES, about 1½ miles, arriving about 11.0.a.m. After settling into billets, Battalion Drill was held in the fields outside the Village. The day was bitterly cold.	
BONNIERES	Nov. 18th.		The Battalion paraded at 11-30.a.m. and proceeded to BOUQUEMAISON. It poured all the way the roads were bad, the same difficulty being experienced in getting the transport over in places. BOUQUEMAISON was reached about 2-0.p.m. Billets were difficult to get as the 40th Division are moving in tomorrow.	
BOUQUEMAISON.	Nov. 19th		The 40th Divisional Headquarters came here today, and rather crowded us out of billets. The Battalion did company training and Battalion Drill. A & B Companies practised taking tools from a dump and filing on to a task, from 6 to 8.0.p.m.	
"	Nov. 20th.		Company Training all day. We are now practicing "TRENCH TO TRENCH ATTACK" and Artillery Formation. C.O. returned to Battalion.	
"	Nov. 21st.		Company Training which was however interfered with by thick fogs and cold mists. Orders received to BEAUVAL tomorrow. General leave started on the 19th inst, and the following have gone on leave :- Capt.O.D.Morris. 19th Nov. Lieut.A.G.Osborn. 19th " Lieut.Albutt J. 20th " Capt.H.C.Lloyd. 21st " " T.O.Jones. 21st " 2nd Lt.H.J.Brown. 21st " Lt.D.R.Williams. 22nd " R.S.M.H.J Vetcher. 19th "	
"	Nov. 22nd.		The Battalion paraded at 9-15.a.m. and proceeded to BEAUVAL, arriving there at 1-30 a.m. The Billets were very good, C.S.M Codling went on leave.	

Army Form C. 2118.

WAR DIARY
or
INTELLIGENCE SUMMARY.
(Erase heading not required.)

Instructions regarding War Diaries and Intelligence Summaries are contained in F.S. Regs., Part II. and the Staff Manual respectively. Title pages will be prepared in manuscript.

Place	Date	Hour	Summary of Events and Information	Remarks and references to Appendices
BEAUVAL.	Nov. 23rd		The Battalion paraded at 8-20 and marched to ST.LEGER-LES-DOMARTS, arriving there at 1.p.m. The billets were quite good, and unusually large numbers of men;12- fell out, and Battalion Orders were published on the subject. Nov.24th.	
ST.LEGER	Nov. 24th.		The Battalion paraded at 7-45.a.m. and marched to BUIGNY-LES-ABBEE, about 13½ miles, arriving there at 1.p.m. No men fell out, though part of the road was in a very bad condition. The Billets here are poor and very crowded. The inhabitants say that the Australians have been in before us, and did not make things pleasant, hence there is some disinclination to allow Officers and men to be billeted. 2nd Lieut.Pollock went on leave.	
BUIGNY-LES-ABBEE.	Nov. 25th		Rain all day which prevented training. Orderly Room Sergt H.E.Moore went on leave. A Draft of 20 men arrived in the evening from ROUEN, mostly from the 13th.S.W.B.	
BUIGNY.	Nov. 26th		The Billets being very crowded and poor, we paraded at 9-45.a.m. and marched to PONT REMY, about 5 kilometres away, arriving there at 11-0.a.m. Here the billets are excellent, and the Headquarters are billeted in the CHATEAU. A very fine old building with splendid furniture hangings and pictures.	
PONT REMY	"		The men are mostly billeted in large stores and factories and are quite comfortable. Training Fields were located and a Programme got out for tomorrow. Lieut.J.R.Symes and C.S.M.Tomlinson went on leave.	
"	Nov. 27th.		The C.O. being in command of troops in PONT REMY, is made responsible for the sanitation and cleanliness of the town. 2nd Lieut.J.B.Greaves was appointed Acting Town Major, and instructed to proceed with his duties. The day was devoted to Compny Training and in the evening, the C.O. gave a Lecture in the Schoolroom to the N.C.Os and Officers on the Programme of Training to be carried out by the Battalion while the Division is on rest. 2nd Lieut.F.S.Green proceeded on leave.	
"	Nov 28th		The Battalion carried on Coy Training all day, but thick mist & cold made work difficult. In the evening the C.O. lectured to Officers & N.C.Os on Training Programme. Major B.F.Murphy proceeded to MONFLIERS to act as the Commandant of the 119th Brigade School of Instruction for Officers & N.C.Os.	
"	29th		Coys carried on Coy Training. A rifle range was selected and targets constructed. The Divl. G.O.C. paid a visit to the Coys while training. Weather cold.	

Army Form C. 2118.

WAR DIARY
or
INTELLIGENCE SUMMARY.

(Erase heading not required.)

— 5 —

Instructions regarding War Diaries and Intelligence Summaries are contained in F. S. Regs., Part II. and the Staff Manual respectively. Title pages will be prepared in manuscript.

Place	Date	Hour	Summary of Events and Information	Remarks and references to Appendices
PONT REMY	Nov 30th		Coy Training all day. "A" Coy fired on the 100 yards range and Bathed in the afternoon. Programme of Training was got out and sent to the Division.	

Alexander Wolfe Lieut. Colonel,
Comdg. 12th Bn. South Wales Borderers.

119th Brigade.

40th Division.

12th BATTALION

SOUTH WALES BORDERERS

DECEMBER 1916.

WAR DIARY or INTELLIGENCE SUMMARY.

Army Form C. 2118.

Place	Date	Hour	Summary of Events and Information	Remarks and references to Appendices
Pont Remy.	Dec. 1st		Coy training all day F.G.C.M. on 20 men of "D" Coy for disobeying an order to fall in on defaulters parade. Capt.O.D.Morris reported off leave.	
	2nd.		Coy Training with Gas Helmet Drill & kit inspection in the morning. In the afternoon Football was played. "B" Coy beat "A" Coy of the R.E.'s by 6-0. R.S.M.Vatcher reported back off leave.	
	3rd.		Sunday, the C.of E.Church parade but one for Nonconformists and R.C.'s In the afternoon promulgation of the F.G.C.M. for disobeying an order and the C.O. read out Sections 4 to 44 of the Army Act Lieut.A.G.Osborn Lieut.J.Albutt,Capt.A.C.Lloyd & Capt.T.O.Jones reported from leave.	
	4th		Coy training was carried out all day and range practice. Lewis Gunners also fired and Capt.T.O. Jones took a party in revolver shooting. In the eving the C.O. gave a lecture, and all the Coys did rapid loading by night from 7.30 to 8.30. 2nd Lieut H.J.Brown reported from leave and the C.O. handed him the Military Cross Ribbon, which has just been awarded to him. The 40th D.R.O. recording the award is No.820. dated 3/12/1916. MILITARY CROSS. The General Officer Commanding in Chief, has awarded the Military Cross to, 2nd Lieut H.J.Brown. 12th (S) Bn.South Wales Borderers. For the following act of gallantry :- On the night of 25/26 September 1916. 2nd Lieut H.J.Brown took part in a raid in charge of a support party. The raiders were led by 2nd Lieut H.S.Wingard and succesded in entering the enemy trenches. Owing to an explosion in the trench, 2nd Lieut Wingard and Sergt Nelson were severely wounded and Private James was killed. 2nd Lieut Brown then took command of the raiders and after the party had returned to our trenches discovered that 2nd Lieut Wingard and two others were missing. He went out with a party and brought 2nd Lieut Wingard in, and went out a second time alone and brought Sergt Nelson in, and hearing that Pte James was still missing, went out a third time alone and found him in the enemy wire and carried him as far as our own wire. The above was carried out under machine gun and rifle fire, and 2nd Lieut Brown behaved throughout with great coolness and courage.	
	5th		Coy Training all day.	
	6th.		C.O.inspected the Battalion in full marching order in the afternoon as a preliminary for tomorrow.	

Army Form C. 2118.

WAR DIARY
or
INTELLIGENCE SUMMARY.
(Erase heading not required.)

Instructions regarding War Diaries and Intelligence Summaries are contained in F. S. Regs. Part II. and the Staff Manual respectively. Title pages will be prepared in manuscript.

Place	Date	Hour	Summary of Events and Information	Remarks and references to Appendices
	Dec. 7th		The G.O.C. Inspected the Battalion on the Training fields. The men presented a very smart appearance and the G.O.C. expressed himself as very satisfied with the parade. "A" Coy bathed in the afternoon and all Coys practised Frost bite drill.	
	8th		Coy Drill. B,C,& D Coys bathed. Rain prevents much drill until afternoon. Orders received for transport to move tomorrow to Camps 12 & 13 near BRAY in the XVTH Corps middle area. During the week the Bombing Officer has put all the Bn & Coy Bombers through a course of bombing. The Snipers and sharpshooters have done special shooting and all coys have fired on the range.	
	9th		The Transport and personnel will have gun carts and Furbers marched off at 8.0.a.m. for the forward area. The total strength of the party being 100.	
	10th		The Battalion left Pont Remy this morning and proceeded to the forward area (Camp No.12 CHIPILLY) Billets were cleared up, the men were paraded and the Battalion marched to PONT REMY STATION, there entraining for "EDGEHILL". The train, which carried also the 18th Welsh, and 119th A.G.Coy was under the command of the C.O. Lieut-Col. E.A.Pope. Pont Remy Station was left about 8-30.a.m. and "EDGEHILL" reached about noon. Upon detraining all ranks had a meal and then marched to No.12 Camp, a distance of about 5½ miles. The Camp had been vacated by French Troops, who had left the area in a most untidy and unsanitary condition, but in spite of this and of the poor accommodation, and great amount of mud, both Officers and men settled down cheerfully to make the best of things.	
	11th		Today was spent in first efforts to improve the Camp. Latrines were dug, paths made, and much rubbish burnt. An engineer Coy gave considerable assistance.	
	12th		A very wet day. Training was carried on inside the huts. Further improvements were made in the Camp, among others, provision being made for a drying room for the Battalion.	
	13th		Training was carried on from 8-30.a.m. till 4.0.p.m. on the training ground allocated to the Battalion. A start was made today to provide a Recreation Hut for the men. The 21st Middlesex arrived today about tea-time to occupy an adjacent part of the Camp. Our Battalion provided hot tea for them on their arrival, and act which was greatly appreciated by the Middlesex, men, and which brought a letter of cordial thanks to our C.O. from the O.C. 21st Middlesex.	
	14th		The whole Battalion was today working upon improvements to the Camp - road-making etc.	
	15th		Training continued today. An application from 2nd Lieut. Mackay for transfer to the R.F.C. was forwarded this evening with a recommendation from the C.O.	
	16th		A Bathing room has now been prepared for the use of Officers and men. Two companies bathed today and to these clean underclothes were issued.	

233 Wt. W 5141/1454 700,000 5/15 D.D.&L. A.D.S.S./Forms/C. 2118.

Army Form C. 2118.

WAR DIARY
or
INTELLIGENCE SUMMARY.
(Erase heading not required.)

Instructions regarding War Diaries and Intelligence Summaries are contained in F.S. Regs., Part II. and the Staff Manual respectively. Title pages will be prepared in manuscript.

Place	Date	Hour	Summary of Events and Information	Remarks and references to Appendices
Decr.	17th		Church parades were arranged today for those men not on fatigues. The remaining two companies bathed today, and changed underclothes.	
	18th		The party nominated for the New Divisional Works Battalion(consisting of 2 Officers and 50 other ranks) was paraded at 11-0.a.m. this morning for inspection by the Brigadier General. Men not on fatigue duty continued training as usual. This evening the C.O. gave a lecture to Officers on Playfair's cypher.	
	19th		Training continued today. The C.O. lectured officers on playfair's cypher and on the attack formation.	
	20th		Fatigues were carried out by parties from the Battalion today at ETINEHEM and EDGEHILL. "B" & "A" Coys used the range and other carried on training as usual. Capt.J.E.Jenkins gave a lecture to Officers and N.C.Os on "VILLAGE FIGHTING".	
	21st		Fatigue parties for ETINEHEM and BELAIR were found by us today. "D" & "C" Coys carried on firing on the range. The G.O.C.Division(Major-General H.C.Ruggles-Brise)addressed the Bn.today.	
	22nd.		We found fatigues today for ETINEHEM and(atnight) BELAIR. Coys continued training as usual.	
	23rd		The Bn.carried out coy training in the morning and played football in the afternoon.The C.O. & 7 Officers went up to reconnoitre the line we are going to take over at RANCOURT and got back at midnight.	
	24th		Sunday & Xmaseve. Church parade was held in the morning.Orders were issued relating to the move on the 26th and the C.O. saw all Coy Commanders at the Mess and discussed the matter of taking over etc.	
	25th		XMAS DAY? The men were given a special Xmas dinner. The C.O.visited all dinners at 1-0.p.m. and make a short address to the men . Orders were got out. In the afternoon and evening all Companies had concerts and the men enjoyed themselves.	
	26th		The Bn paraded on the road outside Camp 12 and moved off at 9-0.a.m. for the starting point on the main road,BRAY, thence through BRAY,CAPPY,and SUZANNE, to Camp 21. The roads were exceedingly heavy. Camp was reached at 1-30.p.m. The Camp was in an awful state and main road in being two feet deep in mud. The cookers were eventually got up and the men had a hot meal.The C.O.ordered sandbag puttees to be improvised in lieu of puttees and the men made these and wore them.Rain came down heavily from one o'clock and continued all day.	

Army Form C. 2118.

WAR DIARY
or
INTELLIGENCE SUMMARY.
(Erase heading not required.)

Instructions regarding War Diaries and Intelligence Summaries are contained in F. S. Regs., Part II. and the Staff Manual respectively. Title pages will be prepared in manuscript.

Place	Date	Hour	Summary of Events and Information	Remarks and references to Appendices
	Dec.27th		26 motor lorries were provided by the Corps and arrived at 11-30.a.m. In these the Battalion was carried to MAUREPAS HAIME where were hot dinners were served.4 Officers and 34 men were left behind in Camp 21 under Major B.F.Murphy who has been made Camp Commandant. At 4-0.p.m. the Battalion marched off for the trenches headed by the C.O. Movement was by platoons at 200 yards interval in the order B,A,C,D. The rendezvous was PRIEZ FARM via COMBLES where the platoons were met by guides of the 1/4th Suffolks whom we are relieving. The last platoon entered the trenches at 6-30.p.m. and the relief was completed at 10-45.p.m. without incident., though 7 signallers were struck by a shell and wounded, near H.Q.	
	28th		The trenches here are in a deplorable condition. The system amounts of a front line comprising of a series of shell holes more or less joined up with trenches. The right & left Coys have no communication at present and all the trenches and shell holes are up to the knees in water. In rear of the front line of shell holes is the support trenches and Coy H.Q. this has no communication with the Front line. Bn.H.Q. is on the RANCOURT ROAD and has communication with the road to PRIEZ FARM and COMBLES by a very fair communication trench Echeloned in rear of Bn.H.Q. are the reserve Coys and dug-outs. The C.O. got out the Defence scheme for the sub sector which was approved of by the Brigade. 1 N.C.O. & 20 o.r. was sent down to the Brigade Lewis Gun Class at Camp 21 with 2nd Lieut L.V.Snelson. During the day there was a total absence of Machine Gun and rifle fire. At 10-0.a.m. and again at 6-30.p.m. there was slight artillery activity on the enemy side. They searched our supports evidently looking for carrying parties. The enemy sent up Golden Rain rockets at 7-35.p.m. 10-10.p.m. and at 11-35.p.m. no action followed and it is thought that they are probably signals that all is well in that particular sector. Patrols were sent out from front coys but thick mist and rain prevented any reconnaissances being made.	
	29th		Everywhere quiet., rain most of the day. The enemy sent up the usual rockets at night. Last night A & B Coys came back to reserve, & C & D Coys went into the front line. The relief was completed by 2-0.a.m. without loss, but rations for the left Coy got lost and did not turn up till 5-0.a.m.	
	30th		Rain again. Nothing of interest to report. Coys carried on improving their positions as far as possible. The reserve Coys provided carrying parties for R.E.Stores and also made shelters in their lines. A West S.O.S.was sent through the Brigade, we sent the message to the artillery Brigade at 4-0.p.m. The first shot was fired at 40 seconds past and by 1 minute past every gun in the Brigade had fired.	
	31st		The usual wet day. Nothing to report. We were relieved by the 18th Welsh. Relief started at 4-30.P.m. and was completed by 7-30.p.m. the last men being on the road to march camp. The men marched out in very good form though terribly exhausted.	

Army Form C. 2118.

WAR DIARY
or
INTELLIGENCE SUMMARY.
(Erase heading not required.)

Place	Date	Hour	Summary of Events and Information	Remarks and references to Appendices
	Dec. 31st(Contd)		The total number of Trench feet in the Battalion is 23. The small number is entirely due to the unremitting care of the Officers and the constant precaution taken on all hand. The Brigade were very pleased.	

Alexander Lieut-Colonel.
Commanding 12th.Bn.South Wales Borderers.

119th Brigade.
40th Division.

12th BATTALION

SOUTH WALES BORDERERS

JANUARY 1917.

Army Form C. 2118.

WAR DIARY
or
INTELLIGENCE SUMMARY.
(Erase heading not required.)

Instructions regarding War Diaries and Intelligence Summaries are contained in F.S. Regs., Part II. and the Staff Manual respectively. Title pages will be prepared in manuscript.

Place	Date	Hour	Summary of Events and Information	Remarks and references to Appendices
MAILLYPAS RAVINE.	Jan.1		The whole day was devoted to resting and cleaning up. The men were very tired and required a rest. A small working party of 1 & 20 was sent to the Brigade Dump for loading in the evening. The C.O. obtained the D.S.O., in the New Year Honours List, which caused great satisfaction in the Battn.	
"	" 2.		Various fatigues amounting to 200 men were detailed and work was also carried on in Camp improving the Baths &c. Capt Whitworth went on a course to L.?OUQUET and Lt.Osborn to FILLIEVRES.	
"	" 3.		The whole of the available men of the Battalion were on fatigues at the R.E.Dump & at Brigade H.Q. In the evening the C.O. went to BUCQUEVENNES North sector to reconnoitre the Line. It appears to be even worse than FANCOURT Right. Orders were received for the move tomorrow to Camp 21.	
Camp 21.	" 4.		The Battalion paraded by companies at 11-0.a.m. and marched off at 200 yards interval to Camp 21 arriving there at 1.15.p.m. The sector of the Camp allotted to us was indescribably dirty, the last unit not having removed their rubbish. Rain fell during the march but the afternoon was fine. Lieut.C.P.Taylor, late of this Battalion, got the Military Cross in the New Year's Honours List.	
"	" 5.		The C.O. inspected the rifles of all the men. Considering that they were just out of the Trenches, they were in good condition. Major Murphy took over temporary command of the 18th Welsh	
"	" 6.		The C.O. inspected all ranks in marching order. All men had a bath and a clean change of clothes. The M.O. had a medical examination of all the men. Capt.C.Morris.Jones who has been acting as M.O. temporarily, went back to the ambulance. Capt.Nicharison having returned from leave Aeroplanes bombed the camp last night but did no damage. The C.O. was mentioned in dispatches in the New Year's Honours List, also the late Capt C.R.Pritchard and the late 2/Lt.H.S.Wingard.	
"	" 7.		Major Murphy returned to duty and was detailed in the evening as temporary C.O. to the 17th Welsh vice Lt.Col.C.B.Hore, temporarily relieved of his command. Church Parade services were held in the morning. 4 Coy Commanders went up to the line to reconnoitre the part we are taking over tomorrow.	
"	" 8.		The Battalion paraded in the huts at 12.45.p.m. and moved off in motor lorries for MAILLYPAS CROSS ROADS whence it proceeded by platoons at 200 yards interval to ACQUIN FLATS. Here we were met by guides of 21st Middlesex and proceeded to ANDOVER where the support Battalion is. Here water was got from the pack mules. 48 hours rations and trench rations had been issued to the men before starting.	

Army Form C. 2118.

WAR DIARY
or
INTELLIGENCE SUMMARY.
(Erase heading not required.)

Instructions regarding War Diaries and Intelligence Summaries are contained in F.S. Regs., Part II. and the Staff Manual respectively. Title pages will be prepared in manuscript.

Place	Date	Hour	Summary of Events and Information	Remarks and references to Appendices
	Jan 9th		The enemy has the range of Bn.H.Q., and the duckboards leading to it, and shell them intermittently, all day with 5.9 & 4.2. The Front Line does not appear to be much shelled. Patrols were sent out and joined up with A & B H on our left and the 17th Welsh on the right and also explored NO MAN'S LAND and found the enemy 200 yards away. NO MAN'S LAND is fairly good going and better than the land behind the front line.	
	Jan. 10th.		The enemy shelled Bn.H.Q., and the support line vigorously at 9.0.a.m. and again at 4.p.m. and 8.p.m. An internal relief took place, A B & C Coys being relieved by D Coy and details forming 3 coys of about 50 men each. A B & C Coys went back into reserve, D Coy taking front line and support. Relief was complete by 2.30.a.m.	
	Jan. 11th		Enemy shelled our support line and Bn.H.Q., very heavily at 11.45.a.m. and 2.30.p.m. every working parties were noticed in strength along their front, but they formed up again. The enemy has a strong covering party always just inside his wire. Touch was gained with our right Bn., and strong posts and M.G.'s were put out by ourselves and the 17th Welsh to bridge the gap which is there. Work done consisted of Baling our trenches and improving them, also standings. We also repaired shelters in right coy destroyed by enemy fire.	
	12th.		Right Bn., 17th Welsh sent up S.O.S. at 5.0.p.m. and there was an intense bombardment on our side to which the enemy immediately replied. Also shelling our support line and Bn.H.Q., It ceased at 5.30.p.m. cause not yet known. We were relieved by 18th Welsh. Relief commenced at 4.20.p.m. and finished at 11.10.p.m. H.Q., arrived at ASQUITH FLATS at 3.0.p.m.	
	13th.		Bn. engaged in cleaning up after the 4 days in the trenches. Men were very fit and there was a very small proportion of sick. Room at ASQUITH FLATS was very congested as the 17th Welsh were billeted there as well. Some extra billets and dug-outs were taken over from the French and relieved the congestion. Capt Whitworth came back from M.G.Course on which he had been away a fortnight.	
	14th.		The whole of the Bn. engaged on carrying & working parties. The C.O. reconnoitred the Intermediate Line and the Line of Advance for the Reserve Bn to the Front Line in case it required to reinforce the Front Line Bn. &c. 2/Lt.W.J.Williams went on a sniping Course at BOUCHON.	

Army Form C. 2118.

WAR DIARY
or
INTELLIGENCE SUMMARY.
(*Erase heading not required.*)

Instructions regarding War Diaries and Intelligence Summaries are contained in F. S. Regs., Part II. and the Staff Manual respectively. Title pages will be prepared in manuscript.

Place	Date	Hour	Summary of Events and Information	Remarks and references to Appendices
BOUQUI H FLATS.	Jany. 15th		The whole Bn. on fatigues all day. 2/Lt.D.Edwards and 2/Lt H.J.Brown,A.C.,were sent to Hospital sick. Orders were received for the move tomorrow. We are to do an extra 48 hours in the BOUCHAVESNES North Sector. Major D.Appleby 17th Welsh Regt is to be temporarily attached to the Bn as second in command as from tomorrow. Capt.W.J.Brown,Adjutant, is to be attached to the 119th Brigade for instruction in Staff duties as from tomorrow and Lt.J.S.Lewis is appointed Acting Adjutant as a temporary measure.	
	16th		The Bn.paraded at 4.0.p.m. in the coy lines and coys were met by guides of 18th Welsh at 4.20.pm. and then proceeded to the line via AILOVAR. The night started very dark and the relief was not over till 12;20. During the night there was a heavy fall of snow and by morning there was four inches of snow on the ground.The night was quiet with only a slight shelling of AGILE AVENUE during the relief. No casualties.	
	17th.		During the day there was only slight artillery activity and things were generally quiet on our front.Our wire from H.Q.,to the support Coy needed repair in the afternoon and 1/Cpl Baxter,Pte Barnett and Pte Bodgers went out to attend to the repair. A shell burst among them in the support trench,Pte Barnett was killed,and L/Cpl Baxter and Pte Bodgers wounded. Snow is thick over the ground and men in the line were engaged in making dummy trenches to baulk enemy aeroplane observation.	
	18th.		The day was quiet with little activity owing to continuous falling of snow. We were relieved at night by the 13th East Surrey Regt. The relief was complete by 11.30.p.m. In relief,companies marched back independently to MAURUPAS where lorries werewaiting to convey them to Camp 21.-- men were in excellent condition considering the bad state of the weather during the tour.	
	19th.		This was a day of rest and cleaning up for the whole Bn. 2nd Lt.W.Pollock returned to duty from hospital and 2/Lt.A.E.L.Bailey returned from Divisional Course.	
	20th.		We were engaged most of the day in cleaning rifles and equipment and making deficiencies good. Part of the Battalion worked on improving the roads and duck-boards in and around Camp 21,and in making separate chambers for Company messes in the Officers quarters.2/Lt.D.Pritchard was evacuated to hospital.	
	21st.		Bn.engaged today in bathing.Church parade at 11.a.m. in Camp.20. The Commanding Officer inspected Coys in the afternoon in the ir h'ts. In the evening 4 instructing Sergeants from the Divisional Gas School came to examine Box respirators of the Bn.Lt.J.R.Symes returned to the Bn.from hospital and took over duties of Acting Adjutant.	

Army Form C. 2118.

WAR DIARY
or
INTELLIGENCE SUMMARY.
(Erase heading not required.)

Instructions regarding War Diaries and Intelligence Summaries are contained in F. S. Regs. Part II. and the Staff Manual respectively. Title pages will be prepared in manuscript.

Place	Date	Hour	Summary of Events and Information	Remarks and references to Appendices
	Jan. 22nd.		The Bn. was conveyed by lorries at 11.15.a.m. to MAURePAS and thence marched into Brigade support in the RANCOURT Sector at ALBANY where we relieved the 21st Middlesex. ALBANY is much shelled and during the day the whole Bn lines were constantly shelled.	
	23rd.		News came that Col.Jones Commanding 19th.R.W.F.was attacked by a patrol while inspecting his line the previous evening,and severely wounded. This leaves our Colonel the only one in the Brigade who came out with the Brigade. During the time that he has commanded the Bn.there have been seven other commanding Officers in the Brigade. Battalion engaged on fatigues and work in the line,especially on making ABODE TRENCH from left Bn.H.Q.,to right front Coy.	
	24th.		There has been considerable air activity above our lines. This day a hostile aeroplane was shot down by the French over Brigade H.Q.,at Le FOREST. Plane and airman fell to the ground in flames. A swift horrible end in a crushed and unrecognisable pulp. The name of the airman was Lt.Rodes.	
	25th.		Enemy shelled our lines violently during the day. One dug-out in "B" Coy lines was blown in by a 5.9 and seven men were wounded and struck with shell-shock.. The men were buried in the dug-out and picks and shovels had to be used to get them out. Some of the rescuing party suffered from the fumes of the shell.	
	26th.		We relieved the 18th Welsh in the left sub-sector of the RANCOURT Front. The weather has been very severe for long, snow everywhere, and 27 degrees of frost.The result is that the ground up to the front line as well as NO MAN'S LAND is frost locked and easy to cross,but it is very severe weather for the men in the line.	
	27th.		Our artillery was very lively all day. Shelling ST PIERRE, ST.VAAST WOOD and the whole hostile front. A great deal of air activity, but otherwise a quiet day.	
	28th.		Our Bn.was relieved in the line by the 2nd Rifle Brigade. The Brigade relieving us was the 25th Infantry, of the 3rd Division. In completion of relief at 7.50.p.m. our Battalion marched by Coys to MAURePAS and were conveyed from there in lorries to Camp 124 SAILLY LAURETTE. Bde.H.Q.,moved to this village.	
	29th.		A day of rest and recovery. 2/Lt.H.J.Brown, M.C., and 2/Lt.Edwards reported back from hospital, and 2/Lt.F.S.Green was evacuated to hospital. All men were provided with a fresh outfit or trousers and tunics. The weather was still extremely severe and had been so now for nearly a fortnight.	

Army Form C. 2118.

WAR DIARY
or
INTELLIGENCE SUMMARY

(Erase heading not required.)

Instructions regarding War Diaries and Intelligence Summaries are contained in F. S. Regs., Part II. and the Staff Manual respectively. Title Pages will be prepared in manuscript.

Place	Date	Hour	Summary of Events and Information	Remarks and references to Appendices
	Jan. 30th		Training grounds were fixed for companies and coy drill and fighting platoon training was begun. The C.O. gave a lecture to Officers in the evening. Hostile aeroplanes dropped bombs in the neighborhood during the night.	
	31st.		Training continued. Snow fell again during the day, and the temperature fell lower. The Commanding Officer inspected companies during the afternoon.	
	1st Feb. 1917.			

[signature] Lieut.Colonel.
Commanding 12th.Bn.South Wales Borderers.

119th Brigade.

40th Division.

12th BATTALION

SOUTH WALES BORDERERS

FEBRUARY 1917.

Army Form C. 2118.

WAR DIARY
or
INTELLIGENCE SUMMARY.
(Erase heading not required.)

28 FEB 1917
No. 858

Place	Date	Hour	Summary of Events and Information	Remarks and references to Appendices
SAILLYE LAURETTE	Feb. 1st		A Battalion Officers Messs was started for the Battalion forthe period we are to be at CAMP 124. Major Appleby was appointed Mess President. The accommodation for Officers was not good, but the Bn.Pioneers got to work on improving the Mess and bed-rooms. The weather threatened a sustained hard frost.	
"	2nd.		Temperature 20 degrees of frost. snow and north-east winds. Training of fighting platoons continued. G.O.C.Division met Officers commanding units at Brigade H.Q., in SAILLY LAURETTE.	
"	3rd.		Col.E.A.Pope went on leave to England and Major Appleby took over temporary command of the Bn. Lt.J.S.Lewis appointed Mess President vice Major Appleby.	
	4th.		Church Parade in the morning. Capt Whitworth appointed 2nd in command.vice Major Appleby, but to retain command of "A" Coy.	
	5th.		Capt.O.D.Morris went to England on special leave owing to bereavement. 2nd Lt.Brown, M.C. took over temporary command of "C" Coy.vice Capt.Morris.	
	6th.		Arrangements were made for cinematograph show to be given nightly in Camp for troops. 24 degrees of frost.	
	7th.		2nd Lt.Snelson went for Divisional Course to ALLERY. 2nd Lieut.Palmer evacuated to hospital sick. Training continued in Company areas.	
	8th.		A team of the Officers played a football match against the Battalion Warrant Officers and Sergeants. The result was a draw of 2 goals per side. Recreational training in the afternoon including Cross Country Running and inter-platoon and company football under the supervision of 2nd Lieut.MPollock.	
	9th.		Capt Whitworth of the R.F.C. came to lecture officers of the 119th Infantry Brigade on "CONTACT PATROL WORK IN THE OFFENSIVE".	
	10.		Battalion marched out of Camp 124 to Camp 21 near SUZANNE on return of brigade to the line. First company left Camp at 1.p.m. and arrived at Camp 21 at 5.45.p.m. The march was a long one, and as so many men had been inoculated 3 days previously, was a severe test, but only 9 men d fell out,	

Army Form C. 2118.

WAR DIARY
or
INTELLIGENCE SUMMARY.
(Erase heading not required.)

Instructions regarding War Diaries and Intelligence
Summaries are contained in F. S. Regs., Part II.
and the Staff Manual respectively. Title pages
will be prepared in manuscript.

Place	Date	Hour	Summary of Events and Information	Remarks and references to Appendices
CAMP 21	11th		The Battalion marched from Camp 21 into Brigade reserve at MAUREPAS, having arrived there at 2.0.p.m. to relieve the 2nd Berks of the 8th Division. Work was at once commenced and parties for carrying to the front line and for working on new battery positions in the sector were organised. 2nd Lieut.Price was evacuated to hospital.	
	12th.		Everything was quiet and no shelling of the Camp occurred. Working parties were sent to clean the camp and prepare drainage as the frost had broken, and a thaw seemed setting in.	
	13th.		Major Edwards of the 18th Welsh was appointed Camp Commandant of MAUREPAS RAVINE. A hut was arranged and appointed for the new French Treatment of Trench Feet and all men's feet were bathed.	
	14th.		2nd Lieut. Green, a new Officer reported here for duty from ROUEN. The C.O.went to RANCOURT Left Bn.H.Q., to consult re the taking over of the line.	
	15th		At 7½.p.m. the Battalion moved out of the Camp at MAUREPAS to relieve the 18th Welsh in left Subsector of RANCOURT. The relief was carried through without any casualties.	
	16th.		Col.H.A.Pope D.S.O.returned from leave and took over command of the Battalion. Major.D.Appleby returned to the 17th Welsh. The day was quiet with a slight mist.	
	17th		The day was quiet. During the night an enemy machine gun fired a few burst in the direction of our No.5 Post on the extreme right. The front line companies took with 2 days rations and gum-boots.	
	18th.		Early this morning hostile artillery opened a strong fire on our front line, the ORCHARD, and the BETHUNE ROAD. Our artillery retaliated and silenced the enemy fire.	
	19th.		The continuous thaw of the last few days has restored the ground behind our front as well as NO MAN'S LAND to the boggy condition prevalent before the frost, so that patrol work was very difficult.	
	20th		The Battalion was on fatigue work in co-operation with the R.E.'s, this included carrying parties to the front line, camouflage work on M.G.emplacements and xxx digging of new gun-pits.	

Army Form C. 2118.

WAR DIARY
or
INTELLIGENCE SUMMARY.
(Erase heading not required.)

*Instructions regarding War Diaries and Intelligence Summaries are contained in F.S. Regs., Part II. and the Staff Manual respectively. Title pages will be prepared in manuscript.

Place	Date	Hour	Summary of Events and Information	Remarks and references to Appendices
	21st.		The Battalion was relieved at ALBANY by the 13th Yorkshire Regt and thereupon marched to CAMP 21 near SUZANNE for the night. The first company arrived there at 6.p.m. and the whole Bn.was in at 7.20.p.m.	
	22nd.		The Battalion paraded in the afternoon to march to CAMP III on the BRAY-McAULIN Road. First Line Transport marched with the Battalion. The Camp was found to be clean and comfortable and some of the men's huts have beds put in them.	
	23rd.		This was a day of rest and cleaning up, all men were engaged on their equipment, rifles and clothing and Lewis Guns and magazines were cleaned. 2nd Lt.W.E.G.Howell returned to duty after 2 months on the instructing staff at STAPLES school for reinforcements.	
	24th.		The Battalion.paraded at 10.a.m. with first line transport to march to BihAIR Camp on the BRAY-CORBIE Road. Companies proceeded at 200 yards interval. The Camp is at the railhead.	
	25th.		Railway and other fatigues occupy all companies today. 2nd Lieut.Weston a new officer, reported, for duty and was sent to "D" Coy.	
	26th.		Capt.T.O.Jones. returned to duty from Divisional Coy and 2nd Lieut.Howell sent as substitute. In the evening a concert party of the A.S.C. gave a performance at the Camp.	
	27th.		Capt.O.D.Morris returned from special leave from England and took over command of "C" Coy.2nd Lieut.J.B.Greaves appointed Signalling Officer, started training new class as numerous casualties in the signal section had greatly decreased their strength.	
	28th.		The whole Battalion with the exception of Signallers and snipers are on fatigue today at BRAY. Special training of signallers and snipers continued.	

Alexander
Lieut-Colonel.
Commanding 12th.Bn.South Wales Borderers.

119th Brigade.
40th Division.

12th BATTALION

SOUTH WALES BORDERERS

MARCH 1917.

Army Form C. 2118

WAR DIARY
or
INTELLIGENCE SUMMARY
(Erase heading not required.)

Instructions regarding War Diaries and Intelligence Summaries are contained in F.S. Regs., Part II. and the Staff Manual respectively. Title Pages will be prepared in manuscript.

Place	Date	Hour	Summary of Events and Information	Remarks and references to Appendices
BELAIR.	1st March.1917.		The Adjutant inspected the Mobilization equipment of all companies, and Headquarters. Orders were received that in view of the enemy retirement on the front, equipment should be got ready for an advance, and preparations made for disposing of all superfluous kit.	
	2nd.		Lieut.A.G.Osborn returned to duty from the Army School for company commanders, at FLIXECOURT., He was attached to "A" Company.	
	3rd.		The Battalion was engaged on fatigue of unloading coal, and stone trains at railhead.	
	4th.		50 other ranks of the Divisional works Battalion were sent for work to BELALR, and were attached to this Unit for accommodation. Battalion again engaged on unloading fatigue.	
	5th.		Company Commanders inspected Companies preparatory to a move. Companies marched to BRAY for foot bath treatment against trench feet.	
	6th.		Battalion paraded at 11.0.a.m. on road outside Camp to march to SUZANNE area, Camp 19. First company arrived in Camp at 2.p.m., remainder following at 200 yards interval. Dinners were served on arrival. The Quartermaster went to FRISE BEND to take over stores in SOUTH CLERY Sector.	
	7th.		Company Commanders and I.O. rode to CLERY & SOUTH Sector left Battalion, right Brigade; to reconnoitre the line and arrange relief for the following day. The Battalion paraded at 10.45.a.m. to march to FRISE BEND where they relieved the 1/5th Scottish Rifles in CLERY., Brigade Reserve.	
	8th.		Two companies were according to defence scheme were disposed of as follows :- "A" Company in the second line at WURZEL AVENUE and "B" Company at OAMIECOURT-SUR-SOMME. On this night C.S.M.Coulling of "B" Coy was wounded by a Machine Gun bullet and evacuated to hospital. S.M.Tomlinson of "D" Coy was taken sick and also evacuated. 2nd Lieut.G.L.Yorath returned to duty from M.G.Course at Bohoon. The Battalion in the evening marched to SOUTH CLERY sector to relieve the 2nd R.M.F. in the front line. Guides were waiting at 6.p.m. at the junction of WURZEL AVENUE and CLERY ROAD. The communication trenches were in good condition and a full moon made movements easy, so that the relief was completed by 10.50.p.m	
	9th.		In this sector the trenches were continuous and generally in a fair condition. Enemy wire was as usual very thick and our own moderate. The enemy had a number of rifle grenade and aerial dart batteries and trench mortars which did considerable mischief to our trenches. At night our patrols were busy wiring, reconnoitring no man's land and exploring enemy wire and positions. No hostile patrols encountered.	

Army Form C. 2118

Instructions regarding War Diaries and Intelligence Summaries are contained in F.S. Regs., Part II. and the Staff Manual respectively. Title Pages will be prepared in manuscript.

WAR DIARY
or
INTELLIGENCE SUMMARY
(Erase heading not required.)

Place	Date	Hour	Summary of Events and Information	Remarks and references to Appendices
CLERY.	10th.		A trench mortar shell had a direct hit on our "A" Coy Headquarters killing one and wounding three Officers servants, also wounding a gas sentry outside. Enemy were using gas shells against us periodically, both lachrymatory and poisonous. These were specially directed on roads and trenches leading to the line.	
	11th.		Enemy aerial dart killed one of our "D" Coy men in a sap head, otherwise this was a fairly quiet day.	
	12th.		An inter-battalion relief took place, and we were relieved by the 18th Welsh. The night was very dark and after two days of but slight rain, the trenches were in an exceedingly bad condition. Consequently the relief was very late and not completed until 6.0.a.m. on the 13th.	
	13th.		On completion of relief our Battalion moved into Brigade reserve, A & C Coys being at FRISE BEND, and B & D Coys at OMIECOURT and in the 2nd line.	
	14th.		Lieut.D.R.Williams returned to duty from hospital, and took over duties of Battalion L.G.O. The Battalion was engaged on cleaning up after tour of the line.	
	15th.		Our Battalion was relieved from Brigade reserve by the 21st Middlesex Regt. Following relief, companies marched independently to Camp 17 in SUZANNE Area.	
	16th.		Two new officers, 2nd Lieut.J.M.W.Barker and 2nd Lieut.F.W.Pozzi of the R.W.F.reported to us for duty. The first was attached to "A" Coy and the second to "D" Company.	
	17th.		The Battalion moved from Camp 17 to Camp 21 on the SUZANNE-MARICOURT Rd. The C.O. went with Col.Bryant of the 17th Welsh Regt to reconnoitre BOUCHAVESNES VALLEY and Battalion position in case of an advance.	
	18th.		From this date, the Battalion together with the 19th R.W.F.was taken on corps duties for building of railways, necessitated by enemy retirement on this front. Work was commenced at 7.30. a.m. at MARICOURT.	
	19th.		The Battalion on new railroad construction at MARICOURT WOOD. The railway is going to be extended as far as PERONNE. 2nd Lieut.Howell reported for duty from the Divisional Recruit Company.	
	20th.		Battalion on railroad work to day. We excavated through the old trench line and came across many dug-outs. Lieut.J.S.Lewis is appointed 2nd in command of "D" Coy and Lieut.W.J.Williams Sniping Officer, is taking over Lieut.Lewis's duties of Intelligence Officer.	

1875 Wt. W593/826 1,000,000 4/15 J.B.C. & A. A.D.S.S./Forms/C. 2118.

Army Form C. 2118

WAR DIARY
or
INTELLIGENCE SUMMARY
(Erase heading not required.)

Instructions regarding War Diaries and Intelligence Summaries are contained in F. S. Regs., Part II. and the Staff Manual respectively. Title Pages will be prepared in manuscript.

Place	Date	Hour	Summary of Events and Information	Remarks and references to Appendices
CAMP 21	21st.		Battalion still on railroad work.	
	22nd.		2nd Lieut.H.R.Hill reported for duty from hospital. The Col.& Adjutant rode up to visit the old German line outside CLERY and also visited PERONNE, which place had only been evacuated by the Germans a few days previously and were amazed at the wilful destruction of property. Battalion still on railroad work.	
	23rd		Battalion on same work ..,i.e. railroads. Things very quiet.	
	24th.		2nd Lieut.F.M.MORGAN & 2nd Lieut.F.A.P.Ellis reported for duty., and were posted to A & B Coys respectively. 2nd Lieut Francis, Transport Officer, was evacuated to hospital sick. 2nd Lieut. H.J.BROWN.,M.C. is carrying on with the duties. It has been a clear, cloudless spring day. Every available Officer, N.C.O. & men were on railway work today, and quite good work was gone through	
	25th		Orders arrived early this morning for a move into dug-outs at LITTLEDALE BARRACKS. Battalion moved off at 11.30.a.m. and took the SUZANNE-FRISE-CLERY Rd. Dinners were arranged for the men at FUILLIERS and arrived at destination at about 5.p.m. Accommodation for men good and ample but Officers quite indifferent. Battalion H.Q., are fairly cosy.	
LITTLEDALE BARRACKS	26th.		Battalion on road work all day. 2 Officers per company were sent. The remaining Officers formed a class under Capt. A.A.Whitworth for general instruction. We have to supply daily salvage sections for the line recently vacated. An Officer of the Lincolns was discovered dead in a shell hole.	
	27th.		Today all Officers were on fatigue. It's a very monotonous job from 7.30.a.m. until 4.30.p.m. and Officers and men are looking forward to the line again. 2nd Lieut.F.W.HOBBS, a new Officer, reported here for duty, and was posted to "C" Coy.	
	28th.		2nd Lieut.G.L.Yorath left for ASQUITH FLATS., to act as Bombing Instructor at the New Brigade School formed here. 2nd Lieut.C.A.WESTON and 2nd Lieut.HOBBS left for the same place to attend a Course in Bombing & Machine Guns respectively. Battalion doing good work on roads.	

Army Form C. 2118

WAR DIARY
or
INTELLIGENCE SUMMARY
(Erase heading not required.)

Instructions regarding War Diaries and Intelligence Summaries are contained in F.S. Regs., Part II. and the Staff Manual respectively. Title Pages will be prepared in manuscript.

Place	Date	Hour	Summary of Events and Information	Remarks and references to Appendices
LITTLEDALE BARRACKS.	Mar. 29th		Battalion on road work. Capt.E.A.Whitworth. Capt.E.A.Whitworth left this afternoon to visit his brother, Captain Whitworth, R.F.C. at ROUEN, the latter having sustained serious injuries through a fall of his Machine.	
	30th.		Road work still going on.	
	31st.		Today the C.O., commenced a Tactical class for young Officers. The Pioneer sergeant started constructing stables. Timber was obtained from the ruined village of CLERY-SUR-SOMME.	

Alexandre. Lieut-Colonel.

Commanding 12th.Bn.South Wales Borderers.

119th Brigade
40th Division.

12th BATTALION

SOUTH WALES BORDERS

APRIL 1917.

Army Form C. 2118.

WAR DIARY
or
INTELLIGENCE SUMMARY.
(Erase heading not required.)

12 S W B

Place	Date	Hour	Summary of Events and Information	Remarks and references to Appendices
LITTLEDALE BARRACKS.	April 1st.		2nd Lieut.F.W.Evans a new Officer, reported for duty, and was posted to "A" Coy. Battalion on road work on the BOUCHAVESNES-MOISLAINS ROAD. Young Officers on Tactical Scheme under C.O.	
	2nd.		2nd Lieut.Peters left for a M.G.Course at LE TOUQUET. The C.O. & Adjt. reconnoitred the reserve line at EQUANCOURT. Bn.on road work.	
	3rd.		2nd Lt.Barker reported back for duty from a M.G.Course at LE TOUQUET. The C.O. & Adjt and Coy Cddrs. reconnoitred the reserve line at EQUANCOURT. Bn.on road work.	
	4th.		Heavy fall of snow all day. Under Battalion arrangements the whole battalion bathes at ASQUITH FLATS. Under Capt.O.D.Morris all available officers visited and reconnoitred the reserve line at EQUANCOURT. Capt.T.O.Jones sent to Hospital sick.	
	5th.		One special leave was granted to the Battalion, so Lieut.J.S.Lewis was granted 10 days leave to commence on the 6th inst. Bn.on road work.	
	6th.		2nd Lt.W.Pollock left to attend a course at the Telescopic sight school, PONT NOYELLES. Its Good Friday. A typical April day. Unfortunately no arrangements have been made for special services. Orders have been received for movement of the Brigade into ETRICOURT on the 7th inst.	
	7th.		The day was used up by Coys in cleaning up ready for the G.O.'s inspection at 5-30.p.m. All blankets except one per man were taken per DECAUVILLE RAILWAY up to LANGTON BARRACKS, BOUCHAVESNES, and there stored under Bgde arrangements until provision was made for their conveyance to ETRICOURT.	
	8th.		Bn.moved off from LITTLEDALE BARRACKS at 8.45.a.m. Companies marched at 200 yards interval. In single file to BOUCHAVESNES, in file to MOISLAINS, and in fours to ETRICOURT. Arrived ETRICOURT at mid-day. Ten accommodation for N Cos and men. H.Q. & Coy Messes generally made themselves comfortable with the help of the Pioneers, in ruined houses, cellars and dug-outs. The C.O. & Adjt. reconnoitred the approach to FINS. 2nd Lieut.Howell granted 10 days leave, and left for CLERY.	
	9th.		Battalion on roads at ERICOURT. The G.O.C.119th Infantry Brigade complimented the companies on their hard work.Capt.T.O.Jones reported back from Hospital, and automatically assumes command of "D" Coy. Capt.S.J.Montgomery (Royal Scots) reported for duty as 2nd in command of the Bn.	

Army Form C. 2118.

WAR DIARY
or
INTELLIGENCE SUMMARY.

(Erase heading not required.)

Instructions regarding War Diaries and Intelligence Summaries are contained in F.S. Regs., Part II. and the Staff Manual respectively. Title pages will be prepared in manuscript.

Place	Date	Hour	Summary of Events and Information	Remarks and references to Appendices
ETRICOURT.	Aprl. 10th.		Battalion on road work on the MANCOURT-MOISLAINS. The G.O.C.in the afternoon inspected the men&s Billets and Officers quarters,and found everything quite satisfactory&	
	11th.		2nd Lieut.Welford granted 10 days leave,left early per Mess Cart to BRAY.Bn.on road work at MOISLAINS.	
	12th.		Bn.on road work in MOISLAINS.Brigadier-General Crozier,and Capt.Goodlife.(B.M.) dined at H.Q. It turned out quite a good dinner. A football match was arranged to be played at 6.p.m. between this Battalion and the 18th Welsh,but owing to heavy fall of snow,it was cancelled.	
	13th.		Bn. on roads. The match which was arranged for last night,was played today.Weather was good.Ground was bad in places where shell holes had been filled up and frequent showers during the day had made these places muddy and awkward for the players. From the first, the team fielded by the 12th S.W.B. was far superior to that of the 18th Welsh.The finishing whistle blast found the 12th S.W.B.winners by 7 goals to nil. The 17th Welsh and the M.G.Coy also played, the former winning. Therefore they will play the Borderers tomorrow night.	
	14th.		Capt.W.E.Brown reported back from the Brigade,where he has been understudying the Brigade Major. The final was played today. The 17th Welsh turned out quite a good team to meet us, but had to no avail. Final score was :-, Borderers 3 goals; 17th Welsh Nil. Most of the scoring was done by Messrs:Evans and Palmer. The C.O. and Adjutant inspected all the horses,several of which were recommended for rest and special treatment. Transport is now being daily inspected by the C.O.	
	15th.		Battalion on roads near MANANCOURT	
	16th.		Battalion on roads. Movement orders have come through late for the line tomorrow.. The day has been wet.	

Army Form C. 2118.

WAR DIARY
or
INTELLIGENCE SUMMARY.
(Erase heading not required.)

Instructions regarding War Diaries and Intelligence Summaries are contained in F.S. Regs., Part II. and the Staff Manual respectively. Title pages will be prepared in manuscript.

Place	Date	Hour	Summary of Events and Information	Remarks and references to Appendices
ETRICOURT.	Apr. 16th		The whole Battalion employed on repairing roads. Major.R.Benzie 2nd Scottish Rifles reported for duty as 2nd in command and Captain S.J.Montgomery,Actg.2nd in command was posted to 18th Welsh as 2nd in Command.	
"	17th		Orders received for going into the line. Men employed on cleaning up billets etc. The Battalion relieved the 12th Suffolks in the Left of the RIGHT SECTOR of the Divisional Front.Headquarters were at QUEENS CROSS. The Battalion marched out of ETRICOURT by ½ coys at 200 yards interval and relief was completed without casualties by 11.15.p.m. The line taken up was the main line of resistance and outposts. Two coys from Q.24.a.0.9. to Q.30.b.5.3. outpost line, two platoons in close support at Q.29.d.5.5. and two coys less two platoons in the main line of resistance from Q.29.a.1.2. to Q.35.a.1.8. The C.O.(Lt-Col.E.A.Pope)D.S.O.) had the misfortune while visiting the line this night to trip over some barbed wire and cut his cheek open with the stake. He was evacuated to C.C.S. the next morning at 9.0.a.m. The night was quiet with intermittent enemy shelling only. Major.R.Benzie assumed duties of C.O.	
	18th.		The day was quiet and all men were employed in improving their accommodation and wiring the line. In the evening Lt.A.G.Osborn took out a fighting patrol to investigate FIFTEEN RAVINE and found it strongly held.	
	19th		As for yesterday. Lt.Osborn took out another strong patrol and reconnoitred the line. Lt.W.J. Williams carried out a daylight reconnaissance of Q.24 and discovered a series of hostile snipers posts, which was noted for future treatment. The enemy appears to be busy repairing his wire in the neighbourhood of TRESCAULT.Sniping was continuous all day. Instructions were received today that the Battalion would take part in the next operation on the advance on the HINDENBURG LINE, their duty being the capture and consolidation of FIFTEEN RAVINE from R.19.d.7.7. to R.19.a.0.8. A & B Coys were detailed for the assaulting line, and C & D as supports.	
	20th.		A quiet day. Wiring was continued. Orders were issued for the Battalion to attack on the 21st inst FIFTEEN RAVINE from R.19.d.7.7. to R.19.a.0.8. Zero time was fixed for 4-20.a.m. by which time all troops were to be lined up parallel to the objective ready to move off when the barrage fell. C.& D Coys moved up to the outpost line at midnight and Battalion H.Q.moved forward to Q.30.b.3.6. All preparations in the way of extra ammunition and Bombs were made over night and the Battalion was in position at ZERO.	

WAR DIARY
or
INTELLIGENCE SUMMARY.
(Erase heading not required.)

Army Form C. 2118.

Place	Date	Hour	Summary of Events and Information	Remarks and references to Appendices
QUEENS CROSS.	Apr. 21st.		At 4-20.a.m. in the morning the Battalion was formed up ready to move off. The following is the official report on the operations sent to Brigade H.Q.:-	

1. In accordance with orders received from 119th. Infantry Brigade, the Battalion were instructed to take part in an attack on the line R.26.b.33 FIFTEEN RAVINE and Q.17.a. At the same time GONNELIEU was to be assaulted by the 8th Division.

2. The portion of the objective allotted to the Battalion was FIFTEEN RAVINE from R.19.d.3.9. to R.19.a.0.7. On the Right were the 19th R.W.F. and on our left flank the 13th East Surreys'.

3. "A" Coy Capt.E.A.Whitworth was ordered to attack and capture the right of the position from R.19.d.3.9. to R.19.a.60.45, "B" Coy, Capt.H.C.Lloyd, to attack and capture the left of the position from R.19.a.60.45 to R.19.a.0.7. "C" Coy, Capt.O.D.Morris was in support of "A" COMPANY. "D" Coy, Capt.T.O.Jones, was in support of "B" Coy.

4. Fighting platoon formation was adopted, each front line company being made up into two platoons for mopping up, with special instructions to pay attention to shell holes, ravines, etc. "C" Coy found 2 platoons. "D" Coy with 2 platoons of "C" Coy found the supporting wave.

5. Special dumps were formed in outpost line and each man took with him 2 mills bombs, (No.5) 2 Sandbags and 50 additional rounds of ammunition, in addition to usual fighting order. C & D Coys also carried a pick and shovel buckled in behind the haversack on the back.

6. An artillery barrage was arranged to be put down at 4.40. Barrage on the objective for 6 minutes and then passed to the German Trenches at R.26.b. and trench in front of VILLERS PLOUICH.

7. At 3.15.a.m. the Battalion took up its position on a line parallel with the objective and in front of the outpost line of Resistance. The men were given their correct intervals, 30 paces for the assaulting wave, and touch was maintained between A & B Coys and between "A" Coy and the 19th R.W.F. At 4-20.a.m. the artillery barrage was put down and the Battalion moved forward. The Enemy replied to the barrage with a strong fire of shrapnel and H.E. also barraged the sunken road Q.30.b.6.2. - Q.24.a.0.0. The Barrage was kept up till 5.15.a.m. and included 15 minutes intense bombardment on the fork roads at Q.30.b.5.2. Machine Gun and sniping from snipers posts was opened along the front of FIFTEEN RAVINE. The advance was checked at about 5.0.a.m. on the left by snipers who were disposed of, and at 5.15.a.m. the Ravine was entered. The enemy kept up a strong rifle fire and Machine Gun fire and only evacuated the Ravine on the arrival of our men. Statements by prisoners vary, but it would seem that the position was held by a strong company of 150 men, snipers posts in front, and supported by Machine Guns. Four prisoners were captured on the Right, about 500 yards in front of our line and sent in at 5.20.a.m.

Army Form C. 2118.

WAR DIARY
or
INTELLIGENCE SUMMARY.
(Erase heading not required.)

Instructions regarding War Diaries and Intelligence Summaries are contained in F.S. Regs., Part II. and the Staff Manual respectively. Title pages will be prepared in manuscript.

Place	Date	Hour	Summary of Events and Information	Remarks and references to Appendices
	April 21 (Cont'd)		9. By 5.45.a.m. all opposition had been disposed of and consolidation was begun on the left by "B" Coy,"C" & "D" Coys. "A" Coy after entering and clearing the Ravine went forward some 300 yards until they reached the enemy wire, the Ravine on the right is not very well defined,and the Os C.Coys were not at first sure that the objective had been reached. This Coy retired on its objective at 7-30.a.m. and continued the consolidation, a party having already been left behind for this purpose. 10. On the Right. the Garrison of the Ravine evacuated their posts, with the exception of 4 who surrendered. The moppers up on this flank searched all shelters and dug-outs. Two deep mined dug-outs were found at R.19.o.7.8. one only partially completed,neither were occupied. A Machine Gun was noted sweeping the road at R.19.C.0.lies position R.30.a.Central was sent to Bn.H.Q. and the Artillery were got on to it and it was actually seen knocked out and gave no further trouble. On the left flank a number of strong posts were encountered between our Outpost line and FIFTEEN RAVINE, the one on the extreme left had a Machine Gun. These, posts were dealt with by our Lewis Gunners and Bombers and the assaulting lines were not appreciably checked. No further resistance was encountered until about 80 yards of FIFTEEN RAVINE when heavy machine gun fire was encountered from Q.18.d.Central.but there were occasional bursts during the afternoon indicating that the Guns were still in position. At the same time a number of shelters on escarpement on the flank were bombed and several of the enemy killed and wounded and 9 prisoners taken. 11. A covering party was sent in advance of the Ravine and encountered heavy Machine Guns and rifle fire from the point of the high ground on R.J.C. On reaching this spot the party found a wide belt of wire behind which was a trench running parallel, with the road,held by a strong garrison with Machine Guns. The Trench appeared to be 250 yards long. 12. A small party of the enemy consisting of 15 men were seen on the left flank,bolting away/from over the ridge. they had discarded their rifles and equipment. Lewis Guns were trained on them and many of the party were seen to fall. The rifles,equipment,and ammunition were afterwards collected by us. 13. The parties detailed as Moppers up carried out their duties as instructed and searched the sunken road on the right flank,shell holes,and shelters on the left. 3 strong positions between our Outpost line and FIFTEEN RAVINE were not disfovered by the moppers up, and the Garrisons of these Posts opneed fire in rear of our left flank and also on carrying parties going forward. A Platoon of the 18th Welsh Regt under our Intelligence Officer, was sent forward to deal with these posts, and the garrison was catpureed by 7-30.a.m. On the right flank a thin belt of wire was noticed running from R.13 a.Central to R.13.d.2.4. but the enemy did not appear to be in any way force here. A snipers posts was located and dispersed at R.13.d 4.4. two prisoners were taken, the remaining 3 men bolted, but were shot down as they were running down the trench.	

Army Form C. 2118.

WAR DIARY
or
INTELLIGENCE SUMMARY.
(Erase heading not required.)

Instructions regarding War Diaries and Intelligence Summaries are contained in F. S. Regs. Part II. and the Staff Manual respectively. Title pages will be prepared in manuscript.

Place	Date	Hour	Summary of Events and Information	Remarks and references to Appendices
	Apr. 21st (Contd)		15. There appeared to be no further system of defences between the pond and VILLERS PLOUICH. From this point it was seen that there was a strong belt of wire running along the 115 contour in R.14 and at R.14.d.3.2. approximately. There was a strong post in a chalk pit, heavily wired, which was seen to be garrisoned. 16. Sniping posts appeared to be numerous on forward slope of spur in R.14. they fired actively along the valley all day. 17. Our own barrage on objective fell about 30 yards beyond FIFTEEN RAVINE. The subsequent barrage was extremely good. Particularly good work was done by the carrying party found by the 119th T.M.B. who under their sergeant carried material from the Brigade dump to the forward Battn. dump all day without stopping, during the earlier part under heavy shell fire, sniping & M.G. Fire. The number of enemy killed besides others seen to fall and carried away, 7, wounded, 16, including 2 prisoners. Total prisoners, 36. Total killed and wounded & prisoners 70. Our casualties were :- Killed, Capt. O.D. Morris, Wounded, Capt. T.O. Jones, Capt. E.A. Whitworth, Lieut. J.S. Lewis. Lieut. D.R. Williams, Lieut. H.S. Green. Killed o.r. 12. Wounded. o.r. 54. Missing o.r. 21. Congratulations were received by the Division on its success. Two Lewis Guns were lost by shell fire. At 9-0.p.m. and the G.O.C. Brigade also complimented the Battalion on its success. Two Lewis Guns were lost by shell fire. At 9-0.p.m. the Battalion was relieved by the 17th Welsh and took up the Brigade Main line of resistance with H.Q., at QUEENS CROSS, relief was completed without incident at 11-15.p.m.	
	Apr. 22nd.		The men rested all day. The Battalion was in Brigade Reserve and orders were received that the 40th Division would assault VILLERS PLOUICH & BEAUCHAMP. The Bn. to be ready/to move at a moment's notice as Brigade Reserve. Weather, warm and fine.	
	" 23rd.		The Battalion stood to arms at 4-0.a.m. the operations above referred to starting at 4.15.a.m. and stood easy at 6-0.a.m. At 8.50.a.m. orders were received to occupy the Brigade Main Line or Resistance from R.25.d.5.5. to Q.24.a.0.0. and at 9.15.a.m. the Battalion moved off to the New Line by Coys in platoons in artillery formation. We were heavily shelled coming across the open but had only one slight casualty. It was understood that the Right Battalion of the 120th Bgde was held up in VILLERS PLOUICH and on arrival at the above line of resistance.10.15.a.m., orders were received to advance and reinforce the 120th Brigade in VILLERS PLOUICH in conjunction with the 19th R.W.F. Orders were issued to Coy Commanders, but before the Battalion could move off, orders was received to stand fast at 1-0.p.m. About 8-0.p.m. orders were received by 19th R. to proceed to FIFTEEN RAVINE and for us to take over the line of resistance which was occur at 8.15.p.m.	

Army Form C. 2118.

WAR DIARY
or
INTELLIGENCE SUMMARY.
(Erase heading not required.)

Instructions regarding War Diaries and Intelligence Summaries are contained in F. S. Regs., Part II. and the Staff Manual respectively. Title pages will be prepared in manuscript.

Place	Date	Hour	Summary of Events and Information	Remarks and references to Appendices
GOUZEA-COURT.	Apr. 24th		At 4-0.a.m. our Barrage fell for the assault of BEAUCHAMP by the 120th Brigade, in consequence this position was heavily shelled for two hours, but no casualties occurred. The day was spent in improving the New Officers quarters. The enemy shelled very little all day, but at 5.30.p.m. started to shell GOUZEAUCOURT and continued for an hour.	
	25th.		In Brigade Reserve in same position. Battalion on our left took BEAUCHAMP without opposition. Men working on trenches.	
	26th.		Battalion engaged on Trenches and shelters. A quiet day with one hour's heavy shelling at 5.30.pm.	
	27th.		Battalion engaged on trenches and improving posts. Very quiet. Working party of 50 men engaged on Communication Trench up to FIFTEEN RAVINE. Baths fitted up and two Coy's bathed.	
	28th.		A quiet day. Battalion bathed and were issued with clean clothes. C.O. & Adjutant made an examination of the approaches to LA VACQUERIE ~~LA VACQUERIE~~	
	29th.		Kept shelling all day. The "B" relieved the 18th Welsh Regt on the right of the line and moved into "D" HQ in Quarry R25.d.3.8. 'C' and 'D' Coys were in the front line 'B' in support and 'A' in Reserve. The relief was completed without incident at 11.15pm.	
	30th		Patrols were sent out last night in the direction of LA VACQUERIE but did not discover anything. The day was quiet except for intermittent shelling by the Enemy and Aerial activity above normal.	

R Rmyin Major
Comdg. 12th Bn. South Wales Borderers

119th Brigade.
40th Division.

12th BATTALION

SOUTH WALES BORDERS

MAY 1917.

Army Form C. 2118.

WAR DIARY
or
INTELLIGENCE SUMMARY

(Erase heading not required.)

Place	Date	Hour	Summary of Events and Information	Remarks and references to Appendices
VACQUERIE	1st May. 1917.		In the line before the village of LA VACQUERIE C & D Coys in front line, "B" Coy in support and "A" in reserve at the Quarry. Our artillery have been very busy all day wire cutting around and about the village. Enemy very quiet. There was much aerial activity during the day. At night the Bosch is still up to his old tricks of burning off and destroying property. "NO MAN'S LAND" has been carefully patrolled by us and we are given a clear field. No signs of hostile patrols out, worse luck.	
	2nd		We are having glorious weather. Wire cutting on the LA VACQUERIE defences is still being carried on with great zeal by our artillery. Nothing much doing otherwise except spasmodic bursts by the Bosch artillery. Our patrols still masters of "No man's land".	
	3rd		No change in the weather. Quite appreciable gaps are seen in hostile wire today. The enemy seem to be very nervous of an attack. During the night he kept sending up single red Very Lights which were followed by a bombardment of "No man's land". Our patrols again out, but encountered nothing.	
	4th		There was a test barrage made by our artillery on the enemy's lines at 4.5.a.m. this morning in order to find out how soon and where would the enemy's reply barrage fall. His reply was feeble, but our ruse served the purpose it was intended for. Our artillery still active on the wire. Patrols still busy. One patrol under Battalion Intelligence Officer reconnoitres Cemetery west of village, but found emplacements and pits were manned., but before returning managed to scatter occupants and destroy rifle pits on N.W. side of village taking one prisoner. The others fled. This prisoner was able to give valuable information re the defences and strength in LA VACQUERIE. The G.O.C sent a letter congratulating Officers and men on the success of the patrol. Capt Morris R.A.M.C. reports back from leave.	
	5th.		Our artillery/still going strong on enemy's wire. Capt Loyd-Mostyn attached to the Battalion for instructional purposes. 2nd Lt.S.A.Sharpe left for 10 days leave. Orders were received from Brigade in regard to operations on LA VACQUERIE Herewith a full narrative of events. Ref Map(Special Map attached in addition to No.1 to 119th Brigade Order No.90) OBJECTIVES. The 119th Infantry Brigade were ordered to raid LA VACQUERIE with a view to inflicting loss upon the enemy, damaging his defences, and obtaining identification and material. PRELIMINARY DISPOSITIONS & ARRANGEMENTS. Prior to the assault the Brigade was located as follows : Brigade Battle H.Q. Q.29.b.2.3. Front Line(Right) 12th.Bn.S.W.Borderers. " (Left) 17th Bn.Welsh Regt.	

WAR DIARY or INTELLIGENCE SUMMARY

Army Form C. 2118.

(Erase heading not required.)

Place	Date	Hour	Summary of Events and Information	Remarks and references to Appendices
	6th.		Brigade Support. 19th Bn.Royal Welsh Fusiliers. Brigade Reserve. 18th Bn.Welsh Regt. The 17th Bn.Welsh Regt. moved up from DESSART WOOD the evening of the 5th instant to take part in the raid. The dividing line between Battalions was the line R.21.a.0.0. - the road junction R.21.b.7.5. - R.22.a.5.8. Each Battalion was ordered to raid with 2 companies in the front line, one company in support, and one company in Battalion reserve. The 19th Bn.R.W.F. supplied the mopping up parties for the Battalions and also a carrying party for the 119th Brigade T.M.B. In all this amounted to 215 men. The 18th Welsh Regt took up a position in the Sunken Road Q.29.d.& Q.30.c. The 119th Machine Gun Co, dug in and carefully camouflaged 16 guns with the object of affording covering fire for the assaulting troops. The guns were so sited as to be able to protect the flanks if necessary. The 119th Trench Mortar Battery were ordered to take four guns into action, and if opportunity afforded, to act on the offensive, and later, when the objectives were gained, to act on the defensive. The 224th Field Coy R.E. were ordered to follow the Infantry and to destroy all cellars,concrete work and such defences as could not be dealt with by the Infantry. The role to be played by the Infantry was as under :- The assaulting waves were to push on till their objectives were reached, and then hold on as a covering party till 1.0.a.m. The support were to form a second line in rear from R.22.a.1.0. - Cross roads R.21.b.7.5. - Barrier - Cemetery and act as supporting party through which the withdrawal would take place. A white tape was laid out from these companies to the original front line. The Reserve Companies were ordered to men the original front line. The moppers up were ordered to destroy all dug-outs and to "clear up" the area passed by the assaulting infantry. For this purpose, the Infantry carried "P" Bombs and the Sappers, Mobile Charges. Major R.J. Andrews, M.C., 17th Bn.Welsh Regt, was placed in command of the forward operations and ordered to supervise the withdrawal. Troops were ordered to withdraw in the following order :- (a) Moppers Up. (b) T.M.B.'s. (c) Covering party. (d) Supporting party. The moppers up were ordered to assist the stretcher bearers on withdrawal. Forward dressing stations were established for each Battalion and a portion of the stretcher bearers of the Reserve Battalions reinforced the stretcher bearers of the assaulting Battalions. This brings us well into :- Dispositions of May 6th were altered "B" & "D" Companies went into the front line, "C" Coy in Support. The day was quiet we sent outs strong patrol at dusk to bring in the few dead we found the evening before, but found the area raided the night before re-occupied by the enemy but were able to bring back two of the dead. At 10.p.m. the Battalion was relieved by the 18th Bn.Welsh Regt.	
	7th.		Battalion all billeted in Houses.Accommodation good.Arrangements were made for bathing at ETRICOURT. Repairing of billets were commenced forthwith. Capt Jenkins assumed command of "A" Company.	

Army Form C. 2118.

WAR DIARY
or
INTELLIGENCE SUMMARY
(Erase heading not required.)

Instructions regarding War Diaries and Intelligence Summaries are contained in F. S. Regs., Part II. and the Staff Manual respectively. Title Pages will be prepared in manuscript.

Place	Date	Hour	Summary of Events and Information	Remarks and references to Appendices
	May.8th. 1917.		Today was devoted to cleaning up and tidying up of the companies generally. Deficiencies were got through. Capt W.E.Brown left for 10 days leave.	
	9th.		Training under company arrangements. were commenced at 9.0.a.m. until 12.30.p.m. The afternoon was devoted to sports. Lewis Gun & Signalling classes were started. New men being trained for both.	
	10th.		Companies under training as yesterday. Lewis Gun & Signalling classes busy. Afternoon devoted to sport. Lieut.E.H.Francis reported for duty from leave, and was put in command of "C" Coy.	
	11th.		Battalion still training. In the afternoon a sports programme was arranged. This included teams, platoons and relay races, high jumping etc. Keen rivalry was noticed between Companies. A concert was held in the evening in a field behind the billets. Officers and men taking part in the singing and reciting. The weather has been magnificent for the past fortnight.	
	13th.		C.of.E.Service was held in the open at 11.0.a.m. and Nonconformists at 3-0.p.m. Half the transport men were inoculated this afternoon.	
	14th.		Working parties from all companies were out at QUEENS CROSS. These joined the Battalion after the move today. At 6-30.p.m. the Battalion moved from Billets at EQUINCOURT to tents and Shelters in DESSART WOOD in place of the 19th R.W.F.who moved up to close support,	
	15th.		"C" Coy are finding parties of 12 men each to work 6 hours shifts under the Tunnelling Coy at 15 RAVINE commencing at 12.30.p.m.	
	16th.		Nothing much of note happening. Companies are finding working parties the same as yesterday.L.G. class opened and short range made on fringe of WOOD.	
	17th.		"C" Coy moved under Brigade orders to Sunken road at pt Q.29.b.25.00. this place being far more convenient/work at FIFTEEN RAVINE. for	
	18th.		"A" & "B"Coys only, now in the wood. These companies find parties to work under R.E.(224th Fd. Coy.R.E.-) at water pipes., horse lines and troughs along-side the CAMBRAI ROAD. All companies also supply men to make up a permanent sanitary party(whilst in wood) of 20 men for the purpose of filling in old disused dug-outs, latrines, shell holes, etc.	
	19th.		The weather is still gloriously fine. Usual working parties were found.L.G.instruction going on daily.	

Army Form C. 2118.

WAR DIARY
or
INTELLIGENCE SUMMARY

(Erase heading not required.)

Instructions regarding War Diaries and Intelligence Summaries are contained in F.S. Regs., Part II. and the Staff Manual respectively. Title Pages will be prepared in manuscript.

Place	Date	Hour	Summary of Events and Information	Remarks and references to Appendices
	May.20th.1917.		R.C.Service held at 9.0.a.m. Nonconformist service at 10.0.a.m. C.of.E.service held at 7.0.p.m. C.O. daily visits all four companies.	
	21st.		No change in programme of work.	
	22nd.		Movement orders were received to go into Close support on the GOUZEAUCOURT-RESSCAULT ROAD. The 2 companies in DESSART WOOD , A & B Coys, moved off at 8.30.p.m. and 200 yards interval,C & D Coys moved independently to relieve the 19th Bn.R.W.F. Bn.H.Q. were found to be the quarters we had built in an old ruined house on the edge of the town when in GOUZEAUCOURT at the end of April. At the completion of relief, working parties from all four companies were marched off to the front line and took over from the R.W.F. working parties there. Working parties carried on until 3.30.a.m following morning. "C" Coy were quartered in FIFTEEN RAVINE.	
	23rd.		A clear hot day. Intermittent shelling of the back areas of GOUZEAUCOURT by the enemy all day. Working parties for the front line as usual were sent up at 8-30.p.m. About 9-15.p.m. a gas alarm was sounded from the sector on our right, but after 10 minutes or so, it was cancelled.	
	24th.		A quiet uneventful day. Back areas of GOUZEAUCOURT still subject to intermittent shelling by the enemy searching for our gun batteries in that area. Much aerial activities these days.	
	25th.		Capt.N.E.Brown returned from leave. Weather still perfect. Nothing much of note happening. Parties for work up the front line as usual.	
	26th.		The Brigade move out today into reserve. This Battalion was relieved at 10.0.p.m.by the 12th Bn. Suffolk Regt,and arrived back at DESSART WOOD at 11.30.p.m.	
	27th.		Inspection of kits was carried out by Company Commanders early this morning, and the rest of the day was devoted to tidying up generally. Divine services were arranged for the evening. Herewith is a list of N.C.Os & men awarded the MILITARY MEDAL during the operations on FIFTEENTH RAVINE during 5/6th May :- No.24263.L/Cpl Alfred Mason, 24275.L/Cpl Archie Freeman, 23714.Pte Edward Thorpe. 23404.Pte Alfred Witherall. 23606.Pte John Prince. 23722. " Joseph Jacques. 23918.L/Cpl James David Quinn. 23706.Pte John Wood.	

Army Form C. 2118.

WAR DIARY
or
INTELLIGENCE SUMMARY

(Erase heading not required.)

Instructions regarding War Diaries and Intelligence Summaries are contained in F.S. Regs., Part II. and the Staff Manual respectively. Title Pages will be prepared in manuscript.

Place	Date	Hour	Summary of Events and Information	Remarks and references to Appendices
May.	28th.		A & B Coys kit inspection was carried out by the C.O. this morning, other companies conforming with the Training Programme. Afternoon mainly devoted to sport. 2nd Lt.E.Edwards granted 10 days leave.	
"	29th.		C & D coys were this morning inspected by the C.O., who was/with the smart, clean appearance of men and kits of all companies, few deficiencies being found. very pleased	
"	30th.		In the morning companies training as per programme. "A" Coy firing on range in the afternoon "D" Coy also fired after tea. In D.R.O. published today, we are pleased to see the following award :- The MILITARY CROSS has been awarded to :- T/Capt. E.E.A.Whitworth South Wales Borderers. On 21st April during an attack, on the enemy's positions, Capt WHITWORTH was in charge of the assaulting lines. By his careful organization of the men and his iniative and courage,he was largely responsible for the successful carrying out of the operation. Although wounded he refused to leave the line, until the position had been consolidated and then only at his Battalion Commander's instigation. :-:- Lt-Col.R.E.Benzie, having been granted 10 day's from today, Capt.W.E.BROWN assumes the command of the Battalion. 2nd Lt.J.B.GREAVES appointed Acting Adjutant.	
"	31st.		Training as usual. Beautiful weather still prevailing.	

W.Brown Captain.

Commanding 12th.Bn.South Wales Borderers

119th Brigade.
40th Division.

12th BATTALION

SOUTH WALES BORDERERS

JUNE 1917.

WAR DIARY
or
INTELLIGENCE SUMMARY.

(Erase heading not required.)

Instructions regarding War Diaries and Intelligence Summaries are contained in F.S. Regs., Part II and the Staff Manual respectively. Title pages will be prepared in manuscript.

Place	Date	Hour	Summary of Events and Information	Remarks and references to Appendices
DESSART WOOD.	1917 June 1st.		Training in the morning. In the afternoon the G.O.C., 119th Infantry Brigade, presented Military Medals to;- 23404, Lance Corporal A. Witherhall. 23714, Lance Corporal E. Thorpe. 23706, Pte J. Wood. 23722, Private J. Jacques. Lieut Symes and 2/lieut Pozzi returned from Daours Course, and 2/Lt S.A. Sharpe & 2/Lt G.W.B. Price and seven other ranks went to Daours.	
do	2nd.		Today is the first anniversary of the Battalion's arrival in France. Captain E.E.A. Whitworth was awarded the Military Cross for the 15 RAVINE ATTACK.	
do	3rd.		No training. Church parade in the afternoon. Weather very warm. Company Officers went up to VILLERS PLOUICH to reconnoitre the line.	
VILLERS PLOUICH.	3rd.		Day spent in preparing for the line. Battalion marched out of camp at 9/30 p.m. We relieved the 21st Middlesex in the Right Sector of the Left Brigade, Centre Division. A. COY on the right; B.COY on the left; C.COY in support and D.COY in reserve. About 2.0 a.m., after relief was complete, the enemy barraged the front line for 25 minutes, and attempted an entry on our left (17th WELSH). They were, however, repulsed, and the rest of the night was quiet.	
do	4th.		Major W. Kennedy, M.C., H.L.I., reported for duty as second in command, and assumed command of the Battalion. Nothing of importance happened in the line. The following were mentioned in Sir Douglas Haig's dispatch, dated 9.April 1917. Captain E.E.A. Whitworth. Captain & Adjutant W.E. Brown. 23563 R.S.M. H.J. Vatcher. Lieut. & Q.M. J. Albutt. D.C.M. awarded to 22729 Pte C.W. Riley 24115 Corporal H.A. Hampton. Second/Lieut. E. Jones and 30 other ranks reported for duty.	
do	5th½		The enemy shelled our front and support lines rather heavily during the day. Two Officer patrols were sent out to investigate the enemy wire. 2/lieut. A.W. Mackay left to report to the R.F.C. Our casualties today were 5 other ranks wounded.	
do	6th.		Quiet day. Usual patrols went out at night and reconnoitred the wire. Casualty, 1 other rank wounded.	
do	7th.		Conditions normal. Usual Patrols. 2/Lieut J.B. Greaves and 10 other ranks proceeded on Signal Course.	
do	8th.		Nothing particular to report during the day. At night 2/Lt W.J. Williams took out a patrol which encountered an enemy patrol, attacked and repulsed them;- we had one other rank killed, and one other rank wounded. Enemy casualties estimated at 5 killed, and several wounded. 2/Lieut Williams and Private Creighton recommended for the Military Cross and Military Medal. Four O.R. attached to the 231st COY R.E. were wounded in our lines tonight.	

Army Form C. 2118.

WAR DIARY
or
INTELLIGENCE SUMMARY.
(Erase heading not required.)

Instructions regarding War Diaries and Intelligence Summaries are contained in F.S. Regs. Part II and the Staff Manual respectively. Title pages will be prepared in manuscript.

Place	Date	Hour	Summary of Events and Information	Remarks and references to Appendices
VILLERS PLOUICH.	1917 June 9th.		Lieut-Colonel R.Benzie returned from leave and assumed command. Major W.Kennedy, M.C., went to 18th WELSH temporarily in command. Sergt Moore of B.Coy was killed by a shrapnel shell T The only one fired at the front line today. We were relieved at 11.55 p.m. by the 19th R.W.F. and relief was completed without incident. The Battalion moved into Brigade Reserve at CAESAR'S CAMP, GOUZEAUCOURT, and all were in by 2.15 a.m. There was considerable rain today and roads were bad.	
CAESAR'S CAMP.	10th.		2/lieut. C.N.Reed and six other ranks reported yesterday. 2/Lieut. F.E.Morgan awarded M C vide 4th A.O. 11.June 1917, for gallantry at LA VACQUERIE, 5May/7. The whole Battalion working on front line (left) digging new trenches from 10.0.p.m. to 2.0. a.m.	
do	11th.		Men rested during the day, aworked night, as yesterday.	
do	12th.		As for yesterday. Lieut. J.R.Symes assumed command of A.Coy.	
do	13th.		As for yesterday.	
do	14th.		As for yesterday.	
do	15th.		As for yesterday. No 45177 Pte J.Creighton awarded the Military Medal for gallantry 8th June 1917. 2/Lieut. H.R.Hill went on leave. Acg/Capt W.H.Howell reported from Flixecourt.	
do	16th.		As for yesterday. Three other ranks attached 231st Coy R.E. killed and four wounded in a carrying party.	
do	17th.		As for yesterday.	
do	18th.		As for yesterday.	
do	19th.		We were relieved by the 13th EAST SURREYS., Relief was completed without incident at 12.30 p.m. during a heavy thunderstorm, and the Battalion moved into DESSART WOOD, the Brigade being in Divisional Reserve.	
DESSART WOOD.	20th.		The whole day was employed in cleaning up.	
do	21st		The whole Battalion employed on working parties under R.E.s. 2/Lieut. W.J.Williams awarded the Military Cross for gallantry on patrol on night of June 8/9.	
do	22nd		Battalion training. 2/Lieut F.E.Morgan M.C. to LE TOUQUET on Lewis Gun Course.	
do	23rd		Battalion training. 2/Lieuts W.H.Pitten and D.B.Powell reported for duty with seven other ranks.	
do	24th		Sunday. Parade service in the morning. Battalion sports in the afternoon. Captain H.C.Lloyd and four other ranks proceeded to 52nd SQUADRON R.F.C. for course of instruction.	
do	25th.		2/Lieut F.Hartley. T.O. granted leave. Battalion on work under R.E.	

Army Form C. 2118.

WAR DIARY
or
INTELLIGENCE SUMMARY.
(Erase heading not required.)

Instructions regarding War Diaries and Intelligence Summaries are contained in F. S. Regs., Part II. and the Staff Manual respectively. Title pages will be prepared in manuscript.

Place	Date	Hour	Summary of Events and Information	Remarks and references to Appendices
DeSSART WOOD GONNEL-/IEU	1917 June 26th		Brigade Sports. Battalion secured one first and four second prizes.	
	27.		We relieved the 21st MIDDLESEX on the Left Sector. Right Brigade, Centre Division,(Gonnelieu) Battalion marched out of camp at 9.15 p.m. and relief was completed without incident by 12.55 p.m. Covering parties and patrols sent out. Acg/Capt H.J.Brown M.C. proceeded on course to Flixcourt. 2/Lieut. W.J.Williams M.G., wounded by a sniper. At night our patrols encountered an enemy patrol and dispersed them. Heavy rain in the evening.	
do	28.		Two patrols were sent out from each company; the first on the right Coy front encountered a strong enemy patrol of about 40. Fire was opened and they were dispersed, and withdrew to the right flank, where they were fired upon by the 18th WELSH, who took two wounded prisoners. The patrols on the left found No Man's Land clear. Artillery on both sides very quiet. Large fires were seen in the direction of Cambrai.	
do	29.		The day was quiet. No artillery fire being observed until about 4 p.m., when a few 5.9s fell near right Coy (support headquarters). At midnight 29/30th the enemy put a heavy barrage on our Left Front line Coy, and continued firing intermittently until 12.55 a.m. The S.O.S. Signal was put up by the Right Battalion, Left Brigade, and our artillery replied. Two patrols were sent out, but owing to the firing were unable to do much. Both reported no Man's Land free of the enemy. 2/Lt H.R.Hill reported from leave, and took over command of D.Coy temporarily.	
do	30.		A quiet day. In the night about 1.55 a.m. the Enemy shelled our right and the Flank Battn sent us the S.O.S. Signal. Two patrols went out; one past the Cemeterynand investigated a sap and wire at R.21.b.05.55, finding no one there; the other to the Barricade on the Cambrai Road, which they found occupied. The Artillery were called on and fired on the party—unfortunately, the Patrol took no further action. 2/Lt. Hobbs reported from a course. Rain practically all day, and trenches rather water logged.	

R. Berry, Colonel,
Comdg, 12th Bn. South Wales Borderers.

119th Brigade.
40th Division.

12th BATTALION

SOUTH WALES BORDERERS

JULY 1917.

WAR DIARY or INTELLIGENCE SUMMARY.

Army Form C. 2118.

(Erase heading not required.)

Place	Date	Hour	Summary of Events and Information	Remarks and references to Appendices
GONNELIEU	JULY 1.		Patrols were sent out from two companies. Enemy seen and fired at at R21.d.4.4. Enemy machine gun fire opened on our patrol returning ⸺one other rank killed, Three other ranks accidentally wounded whilst undergoing course at Brigade school. Artillery quiet. 2nd/Lieut D.P.Powell went on Brigade course. Weather showery.	
	2.		Patrols sent out from both companies. Weather fine.	
	3.		Lateral patrols out. No enemy seen. We took over sub-section B5, on the right, from the 18th WELSH, and relinguished B9 to the 13th EAST SURREYS. Relief completed at 1.30 a.m. Enemy machine guns very active. Considerable artillery activity. Aerial activity. One other rank wounded. Major W.Kennedy, M.C., rejoined. Captain W.E.Brown detailed to act as Brigade Major. 2nd/Lieut J.M.W.Barker took over the duties of Adjutant, during Captain Brown's absence.	
	4.		One Lateral Patrol sent out on left Coy. Three Listening Patrols. No enemy seen. 2nd Lieut H.R.Hill took a raiding party of 33 other ranks and two officers out at 10.30 p.m. They raided Barrack Trench and Barrack Support inflicting casualties on the enemy, and returned at 3.a.m. Artillery and machine guns active. One other rank wounded. 2nd/Lieut E.Edwards wounded on enemy wire.	
	5.		2nd/Lieut E Edwards to C.C.S., S.O.S., went up on out left, artillery gave usual response. Some aerial activity. Relieved in front line by the 19th R.W.F. Relief completed at 11.35 p.m. Battalion went into support between GOUZEAUCOURT AND GONNELIEU.	
	6.		Day spent cleaning up. Coys made concertinas, and three companies provided R.E., working parties, total 114. 2nd/Lieut., W.M.Evans returned from Army Signalling course at Le Quesnoy.	
	7.		Lieut. Hartley returned from leave. Lieut Birkett, M.C., of K.R.R.C., returned to Daours. Lieut. H.R.Hill reommended for M.C. Lance Corporal Goodship and Private G.Crossdale recommended for D.C.M. Fresh vegetables procurred for the men from Cannon. Brigade took over B.H.Q., at R. 31.c.85.75. B.H.Q., moved to D.Coy's area at R31.a. D.Coy moved to R.26 D.7.1. D. & C. Coys bathed at Gouzeaucourt. Weather fine and warm. Working parties from three companies.	
	8.		Lieut and Quartermaster J.Albutt went on leave. A. & B. Coys bathed. All Coys found R.E. working parties. Total 155. Transport shelled, one other rank wounded. Rations not delivered until 2 a.m. Major B.F.Murphy rejoined the Battalion, also 2nd Lieuts Stephenson and Snelson. 2nd/Lieut F.E.Morgan M.C. returned from Lewis Gun course at Le Touquet. Weather wet.	
	9.		2nd/Lieut. Pitten left for course, Physical training and Bayonet Fighting at Sorel. All companies provided R.E.Working parties. Weather stormy.	

Army Form C. 2118.

WAR DIARY
or
INTELLIGENCE SUMMARY.
(Erase heading not required.)

Instructions regarding War Diaries and Intelligence Summaries are contained in F. S. Regs., Part II. and the Staff Manual respectively. Title pages will be prepared in manuscript.

Place	Date	Hour	Summary of Events and Information	Remarks and references to Appendices
GONNELIEU.	JULY 10.		All companies provided working parties for R.E.	
	11.		Luminous sights fitted to a number of Battalion rifles. No working parties required by R.E.	
	12.		2nd/Lieut E.Edwards rejoined from hospital. All companies found working parties for R.E.	
	13.		Batn went into line, left subsection of Brigade front at Gonnelieu. A. & B Coys in front line, C & D in support. Batn relieved the 19th R.W.F. Relief completed by 11.30 p.m. without incident. Patrols were found by A & B Coys.	
	14.		Batn in line. Patrols found by C. & D. coys. Patrols came in contact. Casualties, 2nd/Lieut Snelson killed, 2Lieut Hill wounded, one other rank killed and six other ranks wounded. Major B.F.Murphy wounded. Patrols from A. & B. Coy. Enemy artillery active.	
	15.		2nd/Lieut. R.W.Hobbs, L.R.Jones, and 19 other ranks proceeded to course at Brigade school. 2nd/Lieut Reed and two N.C.Os. proceeded to bayonet fighting course at Sorel.	
	16.		Patrols from A. & B. Coy.	
	17.		Patrols from C. & D. Coy. 2nd/Lieut Price successfully sniped a Bosche officer. Very quiet day in line.	
	18.		Enemy artillery and machine gun very active. B.H.Q. shelled in the afternoon. Patrols from A. & B. Coy.	
	19.		Enemy aeroplane brought down by our rifle and L.G.fire. Enemy aeroplane fell in enemy lines. Patrols from C. &bD.Coy. Quiet day in the line.	
	20.		Enemy artillery very active. Patrols from A & B Coys. Enemy aeroplane driven away by our L.G. and rifle fire.	
	21.		Quiet day in the line. Batn was relieved by the 2 19th R.W.F.. Relief was complete by 11.25 p.m without incident. Batn went into reserve in Suffolk Lane to south of Gonnelieu. 2nd Lieut G.A.V.Humphreys attached to C. Coy.	
	22.		Day spent cleaning up. Coys found working parties for R.E.. One officer and ten other ranks on leave to Peronne.	
	23.		Battalion in training (musketry). Coys found working parties for R.E.. Two officers and ten other ranks, leave to Peronne. Captain Symes went on leave. Battalion in training (musketry).	
	24.		Captain W.E.Brown promoted Major and second in command. 2ndLieut 5pM.W.Barker appointed adjutant. One officer and ten other ranks went to Peronne on leave.	
	25.		Batn in training - musketry-. Coys found working parties for R.E. Batn received draft of 51 ranks other ranks; seven old Battalion men, others new to the Battalion. 2ndLieut Reed and seven other ranks returned from Bayonet fighting course at Sorel.	
	26.		Batn in training - musketry. Very heavy shelling of our area by enemy, between 5.30 and 7 a.m. Working parties found for R.E. One officer and ten other ranks went to Peronne.	

WAR DIARY
or
INTELLIGENCE SUMMARY.

(Erase heading not required.)

Army Form C. 2118.

Place	Date	Hour	Summary of Events and Information	Remarks and references to Appendices
GONNELIEU	JULY 27		Battn in training. One new officer reported for duty - 2nd Lieut A.D.Jones. 2nd/Lieut Thomas and two other ranks attended Bayonet fighting course at Sorel.	
	28		Battn in training. Lieut Harrison proceeded to Divisional Bombing School to take over command for seven days. Battalion found working parties for R.E.s. 2nd/Lieut A.D.Jones wounded whilst in charge of working party.	
	29		Coys bathed at Heudicourt. Severe storm during afternoon. Batn relieved 19th R.W.F. in the left subsector. Relief completed without incident at 11 p.m C. & D. Coys sent out patrols.	
	30		Quiet day in the line. M.G. active during evening, and before midnight. Patrols and wiring parties sent out. Casualties, four other ranks.	
	31		Artillery quiet. Lieut Francis proceeded on Infantry course to III Corps school.	

R. Bunn
Lieut-Colonel.
Commanding, 12th Bn South Wales Borderers.

31 July 1917

119th Brigade.
40th Division.

12th BATTALION

SOUTH WALES BORDERERS

AUGUST 1917.

Vol 15

War Diary

12th (S) Bn. South Wales Borderers

August 1917.

15X
5 sheets

Army Form C. 2118.

WAR DIARY
or
INTELLIGENCE SUMMARY
(Erase heading not required.)

Instructions regarding War Diaries and Intelligence Summaries are contained in F. S. Regs., Part II. and the Staff Manual respectively. Title Pages will be prepared in manuscript.

Place	Date	Hour	Summary of Events and Information	Remarks and references to Appendices
GONNELIEU.	August 1st		2nd Lieut.F.W.Pozzi and 5 other ranks to Lewis Gun Course at Brigade School,NURLU. 2/Lt.D.B. Powell and 10 other ranks to Bombing Course at Brigade School,NURLU. 2nd Lieut.B.W.Hobbs returned from Bombing School. 2nd Lieut.L.Rogers-Jones and 5 other ranks returned from L.G. Crse at NURLU. Quiet day. A raiding party of two Officers and 61 o.r. under Lieut.G.Welford and 2/Lt.Prive carried out a raid on the enemy trenches in B.28.c. A gap was blown by the B.Bs. with a Bangalore torpedo which was successfully exploded at 1.9.a.m. The whole of the party entered the Trench at B.22.c. 20.27. No.1 party took the trenches to the left of the gap, and traversed the trench as far as CAMBRAI Road bombing both entrances to a dug-out about 50 yards from the point of entry. No enemy were encountered in this portion of the trench and there were no other dug-outs. No.2 party took the right of the trench and bombed up to a Machine Gun position about 100 yards from the point of entry. Here they were bombed by the Machine Gun crew and two men were seriously wounded. The party retaliated and put the enemy crew out of action. No.+ party lined the enemy parapet and bombed the trench in direction of "A" Trench.Several of the enemy tried to escape over the top,but were caught by our L.G.Fire. At this stage the enemy opened heavy M.G.Fire on his front line trench from Barrack support trench and also barraged his own front line both with heavy T.Ms and artillery fire A Green Light was fired by the enemy close to where our parties were, and this being mis-taken for the signal to withdraw,all the raiders withdrew from the line. Our casualties were 10.o.r. wounded, 2 o.r.illed, and 2 o.r.missing believed killed,and we inflicted more than this number of casualties on the enemy irrespective of the enemy who were in the dug-out which was bombed. One of the missing men returned to our line next morning	
"	2nd.		One new Officer, Capt.H.C.A.Davies and 3 other ranks reported to Bn.H.Q. The Officer was posted "B" Company. Quiet day in the line. Patrol under Intelligence Officer examined the enemy's wire where raid took place the previous night, and found gap repaired and enemy very alert. On return journey,patrol found one of the raiders posted as missing,and brought him to our lines. Very heavy enemy bombardment of our left front line Coy between 2 and 3.0.a.m. Our artillery replied (Rain all day)	
"	3rd.		Capt.H.J.Brown returned from 4th Army School Course at FLIXECOURT. Quiet day in line.	

Army Form C. 2118.

WAR DIARY
or
INTELLIGENCE SUMMARY
(Erase heading not required.)

Instructions regarding War Diaries and Intelligence Summaries are contained in F.S. Regs., Part II. and the Staff Manual respectively. Title Pages will be prepared in manuscript.

Place	Date	Hour	Summary of Events and Information	Remarks and references to Appendices
GONNELIEU	August. 4th		Quiet day in the line. Patrols from both Coys in front line. I.O. reported after reconnaissance on suitable place opposite our front line for proposed raid.	
	5th.		Enemy artillery very active, otherwise a quiet day. I.O. & Scout Sergeant made a daylight reconnaissance of enemy wire and front line for which a letter of appreciation was received from Divisional General. Our snipers this day claimed one hit. Our Battalion was this day relieved by the 19th.B.W.F. at 5.30.p.m. without incident and went into support, 2 Coys in FIFTEEN RAVINE and 2 Coys near Bn.H.Q. at GOUZEAUCOURT.	
	6th.		Day spent in cleaning up etc. Capt.Symes returned from leave. Coys bathed in GOUZEAUCOURT.	
	7th.		Working parties found for front line. 2nd Lieut.W.T.Powell to B.F. & P.T. course at SOREL. Very quiet day.	
	8th.		Working parties found for front line. 2nd Lieut.Stephenson, J.E.Jones, & W.M.Evans on leave to AMIENS.	
	9th.		Usual working parties were found. Stormy day 2nd Lieut.Humphreys went down line sick.	
	10th.		Usual working parties found. 2nd Lieut.W.H.Pitten returned from 4th Army Musketry Camp. 2nd Lt.Edwards to "INTERCOMMUNICATION COURSE" between Infantry and R.F.C. Capt.H.J.Brown.,M.C. went on leave. Capt.Morris.R.A.M.C. Capt.S.A.Sharpe and 2/Lt.E.E.Morgan., M.C. on leave to AMIENS.	
	11th.		Lt.G.Welford and S.M.Small to 3rd Army School, Course at AUXI-LE-CHATEAU. Usual working parties found.	
	12th.		Usual working parties found. 2/Lt.Hobbs left Bn. for B.F.C.	
	13th.		Lt-Col.Benzie left for C.O.'s Conference at AUXI-LE-CHATEAU. Major.W.F.Brown took over command of the Battalion. Working parties found.	
	14th.		Bn.relieved the 19th.B.W.F. in GONNELIEU SECTOR. Relief completed at 6.0.p.m. without incident. "B" COY in front line, right, "A" Coy front line, left. "C" Coy left support, "D" Coy Right Support.	

Army Form C. 2118

WAR DIARY
or
INTELLIGENCE SUMMARY
(Erase heading not required.)

Instructions regarding War Diaries and Intelligence Summaries are contained in F.S. Regs., Part II. and the Staff Manual respectively. Title Pages will be prepared in manuscript.

Place	Date	Hour	Summary of Events and Information	Remarks and references to Appendices
GONNELIEU.	15th.		Quiet day in line. Patrols from front line companies. 2nd Lieut.Stephenson and 9 other ranks to 3rd Army School for Lewis Gun. Course.	
	16th.		Quiet day in line. Capt.Jenkins rejoined Battalion and took over command of "D" Coy. 2nd Lieut. W.F.Powell returned from P.T. & B.F. Course at NURLU. Patrols from front line Coys.	
	17th.		Quiet day in line. Patrols from front line Coys. Battalion complimented by Divisional General on good state of trenches, the smartness and general appearance of the Battalion.	
	18th.		Quiet day in line. Patrols from front line companies. Lieut.G.W.B.Price to P.T. & B.F.Course at SOREL.	
	19th.		Quiet day in line. Patrols as usual. 2nd Lieut.B.Thomas and 2nd Lieut.Reed to L.G.Course at NURLU. Patrols found posted on enemy wire several copies of "LES ANDENNES GAZETTE" relating to "Russian Disaster". These were brought in and on the following night we posted on his wire our official news for the previous few days.	
	20th.		Very quiet day in line. Patrols as usual. At night enemy used very many coloured lights, nothing followed.	
	21st.		Very quiet day. Hardly any artillery all day. At night All Coys stood to, and were very alert, having received news of impending enemy raid. Nothing, however, happened.	
	22nd.		Quiet day. Battalion relived by 19th.R.W.F. and went into support at GOUZEAUCOURT. Two Coys in FIFTEEN RAVINE, Two Coys near Bn.H.Q. (Relief completed 6.+5.p.m.)	
	23rd.		Day spent in cleaning up and Bathing Battalion.	

Army Form C. 2118.

WAR DIARY
or
INTELLIGENCE SUMMARY
(Erase heading not required.)

Instructions regarding War Diaries and Intelligence Summaries are contained in F.S. Regs., Part II. and the Staff Manual respectively. Title Pages will be prepared in manuscript.

Place	Date	Hour	Summary of Events and Information	Remarks and references to Appendices
GONNELIEU	24th.		2nd.Lieut.Giles reported for duty and was posted to "A" Coy. C.O. returned from Conference at AUXI-LE-CHATEAU. Working parties found as usual.	
	25th.		Quiet day, nothing of interest to report. Working parties provided.	
	26th.		Quiet day. Weather stormy. Lieut.H.B.Giles proceeded to 18th Welsh Regt, on attachment as Transport Officer.	
	27th.		2/Lt G.W.B.Price returned from P.T. & B.F.Crse at SOBEL. Very quiet day. Nothing of note happened. Working parties found as usual.	
	28th.		Working parties as usual. Stormy day. Nothing to report.	
	29th.		2nd Lieut.E.Jones proceeded to B.F. & P.T.Course at SOBEL. 2/Lt.J.M.W.Barker., proceeded on leave. Lieut.J.P.Harrison took over duties of Acting Adjutant. 2/Lt.F.E.Morgan.,M.C. was attached to Brigade as Intelligence Officer. No working parties owing to rain.	
	30th.		Bn.bathed in the morning at GOUZEAUCOURT and relieved the 19th R.W.F. in the Bight Subsector relief was completed at 5-30.p.m. without incident, "C" Coy in front line, Bight,"D" Coy in front line, left. "A" Coy, left support, "B" Coy right support. Patrols found from both front line coys.	
	31st.		Quiet day in line. Weather stormy. Slightly increased activity by our artillery in the early morning. Patrols from both front line Coys.	

31st August.1917.

R Bryn
Lieut-Colonel.

Commanding 12th.Bn.South Wales Borderers.

A119th Brigade.

40th Division.

12th BATTALION

SOUTH WALES BORDERERS

SEPREMBER 1917.

16 X
4 sheets

Vol 16

War Diary

12th (S) Bn South Wales Borderers

September 1917

Army Form C. 2118.

WAR DIARY
or
INTELLIGENCE SUMMARY.
(Erase heading not required.)

Place	Date	Hour	Summary of Events and Information	Remarks and references to Appendices
GOUZEAUCOURT	Sept. 1st.		Quiet day. Patrols out from both front line companies.	R.B. Lt.Col
"	2nd.		Very quiet. Two patrols out.	R.B. Lt.Col.
"	3rd.		Quiet day. Patrols out from both front line companies. Major Brown left for L.G.Course at LE TOUQUET. Capt Symes left for L.G.Course at ALBERT.	R.B. Lt.Col.
"	4th.		Fairly quiet day. Enemy artillery more active than usual. 2nd Lieut.D.B.POWELL was shot by a sniper while reconnoitring our wire in the day. He was removed to 8 C.C.S. and died later in the day. 2nd Lieut.J.B.GREAVES and 7 other ranks returned from Divisional Signal Course at DAOURS. 2nd Lt.Greaves took over the duties of Acting Adjutant and Lt.Harrison returned to "B" Coy.	R.B. Lt.Col.
"	5th.		Very quiet day. 2nd Lieut.C.N.Reed and 2nd Lieut.R.Thomas returned from courses and were posted to Companies.	R.B. Lt.Col.
"	6th.		Very quiet day. 2nd Lieut.E.Jones returned from Div. P.T. & B.F.Course. Major BROWN returned from Gas Course.	R.B. Lt.Col.
"	7th.		Quiet day. About 6.p.m. We were relieved by the 19th R.W.F. and went into support at GOUZEAUCOURT. Draft of 31 other ranks reported.	R.B. Lt.Col.
"	8th.		Day spent in bathing and cleaning up. At 3-0.p.m. C.O. inspected last two drafts. C.O. went on leave (i.e Lt-Col.R.Benzie) and Major.W.E.BROWN assumed command of the Battalion. Capt.H.J. Brown returned from leave, and Capt H.C.Lloyd from a bombing tour as Instructor in ALDERSHOT.	R.B. Lt.Col.
"	9th.		Working parties found. Voluntary services were held in GREEN SWITCH and FIFTEEN RAVINE.	R.B. Lt.Col.
"	10th.		Working parties found for work on new support line. Range constructed by "D" Coy. All Companies except "A" Coy for whom it is impossible, are doing one or two hours Musketry every day.	R.B. Lt.Col.
"	11th.		Working parties slightly altered so that practically all our men are now working by day. Weather fine, as it has been for some time past. 2nd Lieut.J.M.W.BARKER returned from leave and took over the duties of Acting Adjutant from 2/Lt.J.B.GREAVES, who took up the duties of Signalling Officer. Lieut.W.E.G.HOWELL & 2/Lt.G.L.YORATH rejoined, the former from hospital, and latter from England, whence he had been evacuated from LITTLEDALE BARRACKS in March last.	R.B. Lt.Col.

Army Form C. 2118.

WAR DIARY
or
INTELLIGENCE SUMMARY.
(Erase heading not required.)

Instructions regarding War Diaries and Intelligence Summaries are contained in F.S. Regs., Part II. and the Staff Manual respectively. Title pages will be prepared in manuscript.

Place	Date	Hour	Summary of Events and Information	Remarks and references to Appendices
GOUZEAUCOURT.	Sep. 12th		Working parties as usual. Weather still fine.	R.B.W.Col.
"	13th		Weather still good. Working parties as yesterday.	R.S. Lieut.
"	14th		Whole Battalion bathed, fitting times in between working parties, which were same as yesterday.	R.S. Lieut.
"	15th		No working parties. Day spent in preparing for the line. 2nd Lieut. G.W.B.PRICE left for Corps School Course. About 6.p.m. we relieved the 19th R.W.F. in the right Subsector. A & B Coys in the front line, C & D in support.	R.B.W.Col.
GONNELIEU.	16th		Enemy artillery fairly active, but chiefly on back areas. No damage to us or our line. Patrols out from both front line companies. Weather excellent.	R.S. Lieut. R.S. Lieut.
"	17th		Quiet day. Lieut. G.WELFORD returned from Army Infantry School.	R.S. Lieut.
"	18th		Another quiet day and night. Weather still excellent.	R.S. Lieut.
"	19th		Uneventful day and night. Patrols as usual from both front line companies.	R.S. Lieut.
"	20th		Very quiet day. Lieut. J.P.HARRISON left for Divisional P.T. & B.F.Course.	R.S. Lieut.
"	21st		Quiet day. Night noisy with trench Mortars which however, did us no harm, as they all fell in no Man's Land. 2nd Lt.PITTEN left for L.G.Course and Lt.W.E.G.Howell for Bombing Course.	R.S. Lieut.
"	22nd		Quiet day. Weather still excellent. In the evening at 7-10.p.m. the H.L.I. on our left did a raid under cover of smoke. We thinned our line in anticipation of a possible strafe, but this turned out to be unnecessary for nothing came anywhere near us. The rest of the night was very quiet indeed.	R.B.W.Col.
"	23rd		Quiet day. About 6-0.p.m. we were relieved by the 19th R.W.F. and went into support at GOUZEAUCOURT.	R.S. Lieut.
GOUZEAUCOURT.	24th		The day was spent in bathing and cleaning up. Weather is good and all the men are comfortable. Col.Benzie returned from leave. Draft of 58 other ranks arrived.	R.S. Lieut.
"	25th		Working parties found for work on new support lines. All parties work by day giving the men a full night's sleep. Artillery on both sides active today, our own wire-cutting, enemy strafing our batteries. At 7-15.p.m. the Suffolks went over on our right and raided the enemy trench	R.S. Lieut.

Army Form C. 2118.

WAR DIARY
or
INTELLIGENCE SUMMARY.
(Erase heading not required.)

Place	Date	Hour	Summary of Events and Information	Remarks and references to Appendices
GOUZEAU-COURT.	Sep.	26th.	Quiet day. Working parties as before. 2nd Lieut.W.M.Evans returned from leave and went to Divisional Signal Course at NURLU. R/S Lt.Col.	
"	"	27th.	Quiet day. Working parties as before. Capt S.A.Sharpe left for Army Infantry Course. R/S Lt.Col.	
"	"	28th.	Working parties as usual. Weather still good. Draft of 29 other ranks arrived. R/S Lt.Col.	
"	"	29th.	Working parties as usual. Lt.J.P.HARRISON returned from Divl. P.T. & B.F.Course and was sent to Infantry Reinforcement Training Camp at HAUT ALLAINES. R/S Lt.Col.	
"	"	30th.	Day spent in preparing for the line. Weather fine. R/S Lt.Col.	

1/10/17.

R Bunyan Lieut-Colonel.
Commanding 12th.Bn.South Wales Borderers.

119th Brigade.
40th Division.

12th BATTALION

SOUTH WALES BORDERERS

OCTOBER 1917.

WAR DIARY
or
INTELLIGENCE SUMMARY

Army Form C. 2118

WAR DIARY
12ᵗʰ (S) Bn. SOUTH WALES BORDERERS
OCTOBER 1917

Vol 12

Copy kept

Army Form C. 2118.

WAR DIARY
or
INTELLIGENCE SUMMARY.
(Erase heading not required.)

Instructions regarding War Diaries and Intelligence Summaries are contained in F.S. Regs., Part II. and the Staff Manual respectively. Title pages will be prepared in manuscript.

Place	Date	Hour	Summary of Events and Information	Remarks and references to Appendices
GONNELIEU	Octr. 1st.		A quiet day. C.O. went to HAUT ALLAINES to inspect draft for this Battalion who are training at Corps Reinforcement Training Camp. At 6.p.m. we relieved the 19th R.W.F. in the GONNELIEU Sector. Relief completed without incident by 6.30.p.m. 2nd Lt.G.W.B.Price reported back from Corps Lewis Gun Course.	
"	2nd.		A very quiet day. Capt.W.L.G.Foster, Lieut.D.Goodman, and 2nd Lt.W.Goodbrand reported as reinforcements, and were posted to companies. No casualties.	
"	3rd.		Still quiet and weather still fine. Casualties, one man wounded.	
"	4th.		Enemy still quiet. Our artillery more active than usual. Some rain in the evening.	
"	5th.		Enemy bombarded our line pretty heavily at "stand to" this morning. Three direct hits on trench, but not very much damage done. We had one casualty only - a man slightly wounded. At 8.40.p.m. the 18th Welsh on our left carried out a raid on the enemy trenches. During the afternoon our artillery had cut wire considerably on our right, and at Zero, they put down a heavy barrage on this point. Enemy S.O.S. went up first of all on the right, and his retaliation fell on our right front line and support line. Later he moved his barrage along to the left, and subsequently lengthened his range, and put a few shells on our batteries behind. Our line had been thinned in anticipation of being strafed. The enemy shelling was not, however, very accurate, and there were no direct hits on our trench. We had no casualties. When all was quiet, patrols went out and found no trace of the enemy in No Man's Land. Weather has changed during the last two or three days. It is much colder, and we have had several showers. 2nd Lieut.W.H.Evans returned from 40th Divisional Signal Course.	
"	6th.		Col.Benzie went to Brigade as Acting Brigadier, during the absence on leave of the G.O.C. Major.W.E.Brown is in command of the Battalion. A very quiet day. Weather very dull and a good deal of rain during this morning and afternoon.	
"	7th.		A quiet day in the line. About 11.0.p.m the Battalion was relieved by the 10th.Bn.Rifle Brigade, and went back into huts at HEUDECOURT. Quarters were not comfortable for officers or men, but everybody was glad to get in.	

Army Form C. 2118.

WAR DIARY
or
INTELLIGENCE SUMMARY.
(Erase heading not required.)

Instructions regarding War Diaries and Intelligence Summaries are contained in F.S. Regs., Part II. and the Staff Manual respectively. Title pages will be prepared in manuscript.

Place	Date	Hour	Summary of Events and Information	Remarks and references to Appendices
HEUDECOURT.	Oct. 7th. 8th.		Battalion went by bus to DOINGT, where the billets were better.	
DOINGT.	9th.		Presentation of decorations By the Corps General (Lt-General.Sir W.P.Pulteney.,KC.B.,KC.M.G., D.S.O.) in the Square at PERONNE. The following men of the Battalion received the Military Medal :- 23742.Sergt.S.Nelson. 24294.Pte E.Potter. 24202.Cpl.W.Goodship. 24218.Pte.G.Crossdale. The Battalion turned out very smartly, and was complimented by the G.O.C.Corps on the good show made.	
"	10th.		Battalion entrained at PERONNE at 3.0.a.m. for BEAULETZ, whence it marched to GOUY-EN-ARTOIS where it is billeted. A & B Coys are comfortably quartered in barns, and every man has a wire bed. C & D Coys are not so well off, they are in French Huts, many of which are in poor conditions. However, the Pioneers are getting to work on the huts, and will probably soon make them more comfortable.	
GOUY-EN-ARTOIS.	11th.		Day devoted to bathing and cleaning up. Rain fell at intervals all through the day, and revealed further weak spots in C & D Coys accommodation. These however, are being put right.	
"	12th.		Training in morning, chiefly phsyical drill, close order drill & musketry. In the afternoon games. Two of the companies had concerts in the evening. Weather fine.	
"	13th.		Training in the morning, games in the afternoon. Weather excellent.	
"	14th.		Church Parade in the morning, with the 18th Welsh. The Battalion turned out very smartly. In the afternoon there was a cross country run, for which there was a good many entries, and which was run in quite good time. Capt.G.Morris.R.A.M.C. returned from leave today.	
"	15th.		Route march in the morning, musketry, etc, in the afternoon. In the evening there was a concert by the Divisional Pierrot Troupe for the men of the Battalion.	

Army Form C. 2118.

WAR DIARY
or
INTELLIGENCE SUMMARY.

(Erase heading not required.)

Instructions regarding War Diaries and Intelligence Summaries are contained in F.S. Regs., Part II. and the Staff Manual respectively. Title pages will be prepared in manuscript.

Place	Date	Hour	Summary of Events and Information	Remarks and references to Appendices
GOUY-EN-ARTOIS.	Oct. 16th		Training morning and afternoon. After 4.p.m. the Bn. played the 136th Field Ambulance in the first round of the Divisional Association Competition. Our team put up a very good game, but were not in good enough condition to last the full time. We lost 1 - 4.	
"	17th.		Training during the morning, games in the afternoon. Weather fine. Col. Benzie returned from Brigade and took over command of the Battalion.	
"	18th.		Route march in the morning, musketry and bayonet fighting in the afternoon.	
"	19th.		In the morning the Bn. practised attack in open warfare. Usual training in the afternoon. "A" Coy had a good concert in the Corps Rest Station Theatre in the evening.	
"	20th.		Practised trench to trench attack in the morning. Games in the afternoon. Following Officers reported for duty as reinforcements:- 2nd Lt. T.O. Phillips. 2nd Lieut. E.O. Davies. 2nd " G. Simpson. " J. Shawcross.	
"	21st		Battalion turned out very smartly for Church Parade at 10.a.m. Rest of the day was fine. Games were played in the afternoon. 2nd Lieut. F. Eames reported as reinforcement.	
"	22nd.		"A" Coy left GOUY at 7.0.a.m. for the rifle range at COISNEUX. Company was conveyed in lorries. There is a 400 yards range at this place and also a 30 yards range. Some good shooting was done. The rest of the Battalion practised trench to trench attack. In the afternoon we played the 2nd Battalion S.W.B. at Rugby, and lost after a very good game by 6 points to 4 (one goal from a mark, and one try to 1 dropped goal)	
"	23rd.		The whole Brigade did a trench to trench attack practise at SIMENCOURT. G.OC. Division was present and was pleased with the way it was carried out. Rain fell the whole of the time, and everybody got wet through.	
"	24th.		Inspection of the Brigade by G.O.C. Division at SIMENCOURT. Men turned out very smartly and the march past was done quite well. Battalion was complimented by the Divisional General on the good show made.	
"	25th.		Brigade again practised the trench to trench attack at SIMENCOURT. Brigade transport competition took place. Ours was placed second, being just beaten by the 17th Welsh.	

Army Form C. 2118.

WAR DIARY
or
INTELLIGENCE SUMMARY.

(Erase heading not required.)

Instructions regarding War Diaries and Intelligence Summaries are contained in F. S. Regs., Part II. and the Staff Manual respectively. Title pages will be prepared in manuscript.

Place	Date	Hour	Summary of Events and Information	Remarks and references to Appendices
GOUY-EN-ARTOIS	Oct. 26th.		"B" Coy the day on the range at COISNEUX. Remaining three companies did an outpost scheme. The afternoon was left free for games, but bad weather made this impossible.	
"	27th.		Training and kit inspections in the morning. Games in the afternoon.	
"	28th.		Church Parade in the morning. Major.W.E.BROWN inspected all Mobilisation equipment on charge of companies.	
HUMBER-COURT.	29th.		Battalion marched to HUMBERCOURT, where the men are billeted in barns etc. Billets are draughty, and in many cases not weatherproof.	
"	30th.		Training in morning, kit inspections in the afternoon. Weather was fine up to mid-day, but there was a good deal of rain afterwards.	
"	31st.		Two companies on the range in the morning and two in the afternoon. While companies are not on range, they did usual training.	

31/10/17.

R. Bruce Lieut-Colonel.

Commanding 12th.Bn.South Wales Borderers.

119th Brigade.
40th Division.

12th BATTALION

SOUTH WALES BORDERERS

NOVEMBER 1917.

Army Form C. 2118.

WAR DIARY
or
INTELLIGENCE SUMMARY.
(Erase heading not required.)

119/40

Vol 18

War Diary

12th (S) Bn. South Wales Borderers

November 1917

18 X
6 sheet

WAR DIARY
or
INTELLIGENCE SUMMARY.
(Erase heading not required.)

Army Form C. 2118.

Instructions regarding War Diaries and Intelligence Summaries are contained in F. S. Regs., Part II. and the Staff Manual respectively. Title pages will be prepared in manuscript.

Place	Date	Hour	Summary of Events and Information	Remarks and references to Appendices
HUMBERCOURT	NOV 1.		Weather bad.- much mist and some rain. Training as usual.	
	2.		Training as usual.	
	3.		Weather again bad. Training in morning, games in the afternoon.	
	4.		Church parade in morning. In the afternoon the Battalion played the 18th Welsh at Rugby, and won by a try to nil after a good hard game. Major W.E.Brown proceeded on leave and Captain S.A.Sharpe returned from Army Course at AUXI-LE-CHATEAU.	
	5.		Training as usual. 2/Lieut. F.J.Pozzi proceeded on leave.	
	6.		Training as usual.	
	7.		Training in morning, games in the afternoon. Battalion played 17th Welsh at Rugby and lost by 7 points to nil.	
	8.		Training as usual. 2nd Lieuts P.Christensen and R.I.V.C.Thomas reported for duty together with a draft of 4 O.R.	
	9.		Brigade wood fighting scheme in Bois de RIBEMONT.	
	10.		Training in morning; cross country run in the afternoon -- 19th R.W.F. won, 12th S.W.B. second.	
	11.		Church parade in the morning. Captain Foster proceeded to Fourth Army Company Commander's course at Flexicourt.	
	12.		Brigade scheme in Bois de LUCHEUX. Lieut. G.Welford proceeded on leave. Divisional Boxing Competition came off and our man (Private Bright) won.	
	13.		Training as usual.	
	14.		Training as usual. Captain Lloyd and C.S.M Codling proceeded to Fourth Army Musketry Course at Pont Remy. 2nd Lieut J.B.Greaves proceeded on leave. Divisional Boxing Semi-FINALS were fought off, and our man (Private Bright) was knocked out.	
	15.		Training as usual. Weather good.	
GOUY.	16.		Marched by night to GOMMIECOURT, where we arrived about 11.0 p.m. Captain H.J.Brown M.C. left for LEWIS GUN course at Le Touquet. Lieut & Q.M. J. Abbutt proceeded on leave.	
GOMMIECOURT	17.		Day spent in clearing up and preparing for the line.	
BARASTRE	18.		Left GOMMIECOURT and moved to BARASTRE, where we arrived about 10.0 p.m.	
	19.		2nd Lieuts F.Eames and L.Roger Jones attached to the 18th Welsh. Major W.E.Brown	
	20.		reported back from leave.	
DOIGNIES.	21.		Move in the darkness to DOIGNIES.	

Army Form C. 2118.

WAR DIARY
or
INTELLIGENCE SUMMARY.
(Erase heading not required.)

Instructions regarding War Diaries and Intelligence Summaries are contained in F. S. Regs. Part II and the Staff Manual respectively. Title pages will be prepared in manuscript.

Place	Date	Hour	Summary of Events and Information	Remarks and references to Appendices
GRAINCOURT.	NOVR. 22.		Moved in the darkness to GRAINCOURT. 2nd Lieut. F.W.Pozzi reported back from leave. Lieut.H.R.Taylor (formerly Divisional Claims' Officer) reported fr r duty. Orders received for the Battalion to take part in the attack on BOURLON WOOD on the following day.	
BOURLON WOOD.	23.		At 10.30 our artillery opened an intense artillery bombardment on the southern edge of BOURLON WOOD, and immediately afterwards the infantry advanced to the attack. The 19th R.W.F., were on the right of the Brigade sector, and the 12th S.W.B., on the left. Tanks went in in advance of our left company, but there were none in front of our right company. No opposition was met with until we got into the wood, when our right company got into touch with the enemy and forced him back. We continued to push forward until we reached the middle of the wood, where our left company met with very strong resistance. Enemy machine gun fire was severe, and we sustained a large number of casualties, particularly among officers and N.C.O's. The right company reached the outskirts of BOURLON village, but had lost touch with both flanks and could not advance further. The left company, reinforced by one company of the 17th WELSH at 12.45/a.m. by a second company at 1.25 p.m., continued to press forward, but were held up inside the wood by heavy machine gun fire. At 1.30 p.m., it having been reported that nearly all our officers had become casualties, Major W.M.BROWN was sent up to reorganise. A strong enemy counter attack forced back our left company and we lined a road running East and West through the middle of the wood. One company was still cut off in BOURLON village, but with the aid of a tank they succeeded in forcing their way back and getting into touch with the rest of our line. About 3.0.p.m. Lieut W.M. EVANS was sent up to help Major W.M. BROWN — all the other officers of the Battalion having by now become casualties. At 4.0.p.m. the enemy counter attacked heavily. Both our flanks were in the air at the time, but the 18th WELSH came up just in time to prevent our being surrounded. The attack was beaten off and the 18th WELSH advanced and occupied the high ground in front of the road.	
			At 7.0 p.m. Lieut-Colonel R.BENZIE was put in command of all operations in the forward area on the Brigade front. From this time onwards the 12th S.W.B., formed part of a composite Battalion under Lieut-Colonel PLUNKETT, who was assisted by Major W.M.BROWN. Lieut W.M.EVANS was in charge of the 12th S.W.B. in the line.	
	24.		About 8.30 a.m. the enemy attacked very heavily, coming on in droves, without any particular formation. We waited until they were about 150 yards away, and then opened rapid fire with rifles and Lewis guns. They melted away completely, and not a single German reached our line. When the enemy was seen advancing a message was sent to our artillery, and about 9.0 a.m. they put down a heavy barrage which fell short and dropped dead on our line. We were compelled to retire, and took up a position on a sunken road, about 300 yards in rear of the	

WAR DIARY
or
INTELLIGENCE SUMMARY.
(Erase heading not required.)

Army Form C. 2118.

Place	Date	Hour	Summary of Events and Information	Remarks and references to Appendices
BOURLON WOOD	NOVR 24 (on)		line. Here we were reinforced soon after 9.0 o'clock by 2 companies of the ARGYLLS & SUTHERLAND HIGHLANDERS. The barrage lifted about 9.45 a.m. and we moved forward and occupied the original line - the A.& S.H., in the front line, ourselves in close support about 50 yards behind. The enemy shelled our line heavily throughout the day, but we had comparatively few casualties.	305

	25		At 4.0 p.m. as the A.& S.H., who were then holding line on right of battalion, had withdrawn from sunken road in rear Lieut Evans withdrew to a sunken road in rear, but was ordered to reoccupy original line, which was done. At 11.15 p.m. the SCOTS GUARDS having come up, Brigade Details were reorganised. K.O.S.B. were ordered to hold left front line, while the Brigade held the centre with SCOTS GUARDS on right. While this reorganisation was in progress Major W.B.BROWN was wounded by an enemy bombing party, which had succeeded in forcing one of our strong posts. ~~We were able to make good our original front line.~~ Throughout the morning we were worried by heavy machine guns and sniping, but the enemy did not put any shells on our front line. At 2.0 p.m. we again attacked, but found the enemy counter attacking at the same time. One burst of rapid fire completely broke up his attack, and we tried to get on. Six separate attempts were made, all ranks displaying fine spirit and dash; but owing to the very heavy machine gun fire we were unable to take the strong point at the edge of the wood which was our objectives. In response to a message from the 2nd SCOTS GUARDS, who were attacking on our right, we took our Lewis guns and all our men directed covering fire on enemy, enabling the Guards to capture the high ground which formed their objective. All was quiet after this until about 10.0 p.m., when the enemy made another strong counter attack. His advance was observed by our forward posts and a terrific burst of fire was opened on him by rifles, Lewis guns and Vickers guns. The attack was completely beaten back, and our line on the high ground was handed over intact to the 2/6 DUKE OF WELLINGTON'S regiment, who relieved us about 11.0 pm. Our casualties during the operations 23rd-25th November were as follows:-
			
			                   OFFICERS OTHER RANKS
			Killed or died of wounds 9 46
			Wounded 12 241
			Missing 1 17
			                               22 304
			
			(above are figures as known 30.11.17)
				308

Instructions regarding War Diaries and Intelligence Summaries are contained in F. S. Regs., Part II. and the Staff Manual respectively. Title pages will be prepared in manuscript.

WAR DIARY
or
INTELLIGENCE SUMMARY.
(Erase heading not required.)

Army Form C. 2118.

Place	Date	Hour	Summary of Events and Information	Remarks and references to Appendices
BOURLON WOOD	NOVR 25 (on)		Casualties to officers were as under:-	
			KILLED, Captain S.A.Sharpe, (Sharpe) Lieut. E.Edwards, Lieut. G.L.Yorath, Lieut. G.W.B.Price, Lieut. D.Goodman, Lieut. C.N.Reed, 2/Lt. F.E.Morgan, M.C., 2/Lt. R.I.V.C.Thomas.	808
			DIED OF WOUNDS,	
			WOUNDED, 2/Lt. E.J.J.Hooper, Captain J.E.Jenkins, Captain H.C.A.Davies, Captain J.R.Symes, Lieut. W.M.Evans, Lieut. F.W.Hartley, 2/Lt. F.A.Stephenson, 2/Lt. J.Shewcross, 2/Lt. W.T.Powell, 2/Lt. G.Simpson. 2/Lt. R.Thomas, 2/Lt. E.Jones, Major W.E.Brown.	
			MISSING, 2/Lt. E.O.Davies.	
			After relief we marched to the HINDENBURG SUPPORT LINE, near HAVRINCOURT, where we spent the night in dugouts.	
LECHELLE BERLES-AUX-BOIS.	26.		Battalion marched to LECHELLE.	
	27.		Marched to YTRES, where we entrained for BEAUMETZ, from which place we marched to BERLES-AUX-BOIS, arriving there about 5.0.P.M. The Battalion is accommodated in billets, and both officers and men are fairly comfortable.	808

Army Form C. 2118.

WAR DIARY
or
INTELLIGENCE SUMMARY.
(Erase heading not required.)

Place	Date	Hour	Summary of Events and Information	Remarks and references to Appendices
BERLES-AUX-BOIS.	NOV. 28.		Day spent in cleaning up and refitting.	
	29.		As yesterday. Battalion bathed at batas in this village.	
	30.		Battalion bathed and had clean change at batas at BIENVILLERS. Battalion parade for reading of messages of congratulation on the recent fighting. 2nd Lieuts. F.James and L.Rogers Jones returned to the Battalion from the 18th March.	

R R Kinji Lieut-Colonel.
Commanding, 12th Bn.South Wales Borderers

119th Brigade.

40th Division.

12th BATTALION

SOUTH WALES BORDERERS

DECEMBER 1917.

Army Form C. 2118.

WAR DIARY
or
INTELLIGENCE SUMMARY.

(Erase heading not required.)

Vol 19

19 x
5 sheet

War Diary

12th (S.) Bn. South Wales Borderers

Dec. 1917.

WAR DIARY
or
INTELLIGENCE SUMMARY.
(Erase heading not required).

Army Form C. 2118.

Place	Date	Hour	Summary of Events and Information	Remarks and references to Appendices
BARASTRE-AU-BOIS ENVILLERS	1917 Decr 1.		Battalion stood by in billets all day in anticipation of an immediate move, but this did not come off. Capt H.J.Brown M.C. reported back from G.H.Q., Lewis Gun course. WMJ	
	2.		Battalion paraded at 11.45 am and marched to BULLECOURT, where we got into 'buses, which conveyed us to ERVILLERS. We relieved the 7th CHESHIRES (two companies and H.Q.) in DUTTON CAMP and two companies of the 6th CONNAUGHT RANGERS in RAILWAY RESERVE. Battalion is at present in Brigade support, the 119th Brigade being right Brigade in the BULLECOURT Sector. WMJ	
RAILWAY RESERVE	3.		Remaining two companies and H.Q. moved up from HUT 9 CAMP to RAILWAY RESERVE. Accomodation is not adequate, and good weather proof quarters, fit for winter quarters, will have to be made. There is plenty of material available, and the work will be proceeded with as quickly as possible. Lt & Q.M. J.Arbutt returned from leave, and 2/Lt W.H.Pitten returned from Musketry course at HYTHE. WMJ	
	4.		Men engaged chiefly on dugouts. Several parties also detailed to look after dumps, water tanks etc. B. & D Coys found working parties for the 19th L.F., at night. Lieut T.W.Evans and 7 other ranks proceeded on leave. We continue to send parties on leave daily. WMJ	
	5.		Working parties found, chiefly on carrying material and work in communication trenches. 2/Lt. J.L.Barton, 13th Yorks, temporarily attached to us, reported for duty, and was posted to A.Coy. Weather today and for the past week has been fine and dry, but very cold, especially at nights. WMJ	
	6.		Carrying parties supplies to both front line battalions. Work on dugouts is being proceeded with satisfactorily. Weather still fine. Captain H.C.Lloyd returned from front line trench. Remaining men on dugouts and carrying parties. WMJ	
	7.		Part of 56 O.R. arrived. Two companies worked at night on the Army Musketry School.	
BULLECOURT SECTOR	8.		In the evening we relieved the 19th L.F., as right Battalion in the BULLECOURT Sector. Relief was carried out satisfactorily by 8.30 p.m. A. & B. Coys are in the front line and C. & D. Companies in support. WMJ	
	9.		A quiet day and night. Day was cloudy and misty, and the night very dark. We had listening patrols out all night, but they found no sign of the enemy in No Man's Land. Major C.W.Jenkins (Shropshire Yeomanry) attached 8th East Yorks Regt) reported for duty as second-in-command. WMJ	
	9.10		Day and night were quiet on our front, although there was considerable activity (artillery). Enemy aeroplanes were busy all day. About 11 p.m. on the front of the 3rd Division on our right, enemy aeroplanes had reported unusual amount of movement behind the German lines, and an attack seemed probable. Every precaution was taken, but the night WMJ passed quietly and without incident. 2/Lt G.P.Moss reported as a reinforcement officer.	
	10.11		Day was fairly quiet, although the enemy got in many shells into BULLECOURT and about at various times. Weather fine, but cloudy and misty, hence no aerial activity. WMJ	

WAR DIARY or INTELLIGENCE SUMMARY

Army Form C. 2118.

(Erase heading not required.)

Instructions regarding War Diaries and Intelligence Summaries are contained in F. S. Regs., Part II. and the Staff Manual respectively. Title pages will be prepared in manuscript.

Place	Date	Hour	Summary of Events and Information	Remarks and references to Appendices
BULLECOURT	1917 Decr 12	12.	About 6.45 a.m. an S.O.S. went up on front of 3rd Division (on our right). Our artillery put down a heavy barrage along our whole front. At 7.20 a.m. enemy infantry action having developed the barrage ceased on our front. On the 3rd Division front, however, where the enemy had attacked, there was considerable activity throughout the day, but nothing was seen of any enemy aircraft on our front. A patrol went out from our right company to reconnoitre an enemy post at the junction of TALLUD VALLEY and HAPPONE TRENCH. About 9 p.m. information was received that prisoners captured by the 3rd Division had stated that an attack was to be made in the neighbourhood of BULLECOURT at 6.30 a.m. next day. Necessary action was taken to resist any such attack if it were made. Following officers reported as reinforcements:— 2nd Lieuts R.J. SMITH, G.H. MORGAN, H. JONES, A. LLEWLIN, A.M. CHAPMAN, J.W. CLIFF, H. HARVEY, and W.G. EDWARDS.	✓
		13.	From 1.30 a.m. to 2.0 a.m. and from 4.30 a.m. to 5 a.m. the enemy carried out a heavy bombardment on our trenches and battery positions. A number of gas shells were mixed with H.E. and shrapnel. About 6.40 a.m. S.O.S. went up on 3rd Division front and our artillery put down a heavy barrage, lasting for about half an hour. No infantry action developed on our front. Day was cloudy and there was little aerial activity on either side. Both our own and the enemy artillery were quiet during the morning, and fairly active in the afternoon. Enemy put a good number of shells into BUCQUOY, and about 4 p.m. lightly bombarded our front line, doing no damage. Patrol further reconnoitred enemy post at bottom of TALLUD VALLEY. Lieut J.P. Harrison, (attached Divnal Reinforcement Camp) proceeded on leave, and 2X 2/Lt J.L. Barton (13th Yorks) returned to his unit.	✓
		14.	Day was fairly quiet on our front, there was still great activity on our right. About 9 p.m. we were relieved by the 19th R.W.F. and went to NISLAND CAMP, ERVILLERS, in Brigade reserve. Weather was cloudy and there was some rain in the evening. Battalion has been very fortunate this tour, having had only one casualty, and that very slight. Major G.W. Jenkins left us to take command of the 19th R.W.F.	✓
ERVILLERS		15.	Day spent cleaning up. Lecture to N.C.O's by Captain Floyd in the evening. 2/Lieuts O.Hart and J.Pemberton reported as reinforcements.	✓
		16.	A.Company bathed. Church parade service was held at 6.0 p.m. Weather cold and some snow. Capt N.W.G. Foster returned from Army course.	✓
		17.	Remaining companies bathed. Training interfered with by snow. All companies went for a run in the morning. Specialist training in the afternoon.	✓
		18.	Weather still very cold but fine and dry. Training was carried out according to programme.	✓
		19.	Training, frost continued.	✓

WAR DIARY
or
INTELLIGENCE SUMMARY.
(Erase heading not required.)

Army Form C. 2118.

Place	Date	Hour	Summary of Events and Information	Remarks and references to Appendices
ERVILLERS	1917 Decr 20.		2/Lt L.Rogers Jones proceeded on leave. About 6.p.m. we relieved the 19th E.W.F. in the right BULLECOURT sector. Relief was accomplished without incident and completed by 8.30 p.m.	
BULLECOURT	21.		A quiet day and night weather very cloudy and misty. During the afternoon 2/Lt Moss was wounded by a shot from a sniper. Information was received today that the following N.C.O's and men of the Battalion had been awarded the MILITARY MEDAL. 8272 Sergeant Carroll P. 24309 Private Pace D. 23657 Private Townsend F. 33847 Private Cochrane H. 2431 L/Corporal Boobyer J. 41226 " Fosythe S. 24261 " McCormick J. 39949 Private Smith G.H. 25236 " Moffatt C.W. 24043 " Lockwood J. 23724 " McCrann J.	
BULLECOURT	22.		Quiet day and night. Two patrols sent out. Night patrol found no sign of enemy. Left patrol located enemy wiring party, but efforts to cut it off failed. Our patrol was challenged and fire opened by enemy M.G. One man missing for a few hours. He turned up late unwounded.	
	23.		2/Lt J.B.Greaves proceeded to U.K. on leave. Lieut Francis reported from hospital. A number of enemy working parties observed during the day. Artillery informed and parties dispersed by fire. Two patrols found no sign of the enemy in No Man's Land. Major C.B. Jenkins returned from 19th E.W.F. to take over duties of 2nd in Command. Lieut W.M. Evans reported back from leave. 7323 Lance Corporal Ellis awarded the Military Medal.	
	24.		Day and night very quiet. A fall of snow and full moon made patroling and wiring very difficult.	
	25.		Inter-company relief "C & D. in front line. A. & B. in close support.	
	26.		Enemy artillery a little more active, otherwise quite an ordinary day. Intermittent shelling of our front and support lines with 77mm H.E., Gunfire & Plumm trenches receiving special attention. Moon angers patrolling. Landscape still covered with snow. Bn relieved by 17th E.W.F. and moved into support to Railway Reserve. Relief completed 8.30 p.m. without incident.	
RAILWAY RESERVE	27.		Working parties employed, chiefly on new accommodation. Bn enjoyed its Xmas dinner of Turkey, Roast beef, Potatoes, Plum pudding and Nuts. Lieut H.A.Taylor and C.S.M. Carroll left for 3rd Army Course.	
	28.		Day and night very quiet. Lieut E.H.Francis proceeded on leave to the U.K. B.Coy bathed and received clean change of clothing at St Leger.	
	29		D Coy to ST LEGER for baths. Bn finding working parties for trenches and shelters enemy fired a few gas shells. There were no casualties.	
	30.		C. Coy to ST LEGER for baths. The following awards granted for gallantry in the operations at BULLEOH WOOD on November 23/25th 1917.	

WAR DIARY
or
INTELLIGENCE SUMMARY.

(Erase heading not required.)

Army Form C. 2118.

Place	Date	Hour	Summary of Events and Information	Remarks and references to Appendices
RAILWAY RESERVE	1917 Dec r 30.(con)		DISTINGUISHED SERVICE ORDER. Lieut-Colonel R.Benzie. Lieut /.M.Evans. MILITARY CROSS. Major W.E.Brown. Captain J.R.Symes. 2/Lieut. A.Thomas. 2/Lieut F.Eames. Capt G.Morris, R.A.M.C., C.S.M. T.Jones (A.Coy) C.S.M. H.H.Stone (C.Coy) DISTINGUISHED CONDUCT MEDAL. 24415 A/Sergeant H.A.Hampton. (A.Coy) 9524 Private J.Hewitt (B.Coy) 23483 " F.Plumner (A.Coy) 18460 L/Corporal J.Prescott (D.Coy) 23938 Corporal H.Haywood (C.Coy) 22798 L/Corporal J.Stockton (D.Coy) WmS.	
	31.		A.Coy to St Leger for baths. Major W.E.Brown returned from hospital and took over duties as 2nd in command. The following also reported for duty, 2nd/Lieuts. C.S.Woodward, E.Brewer and A.J Hardwick. WmS.	

R. Benzie
Lieut-Colonel.
Commanding, 18th Bn South Wales Borderers

119th Brigade.
40th Division.

12th BATTALION

SOUTH WALES BORDERERS

JANUARY 1918.

Army Form C. 2118.

WAR DIARY
or
INTELLIGENCE SUMMARY.
(Erase heading not required.)

War Diary
12th Bn. K.O.S.Borderers
January 1918

Army Form C. 2118.

WAR DIARY
or
INTELLIGENCE SUMMARY.
(Erase heading not required.)

Instructions regarding War Diaries and Intelligence Summaries are contained in F. S. Regs., Part II. and the Staff Manual respectively. Title pages will be prepared in manuscript.

Place	Date 1918.	Hour	Summary of Events and Information	Remarks and references to Appendices
RAILWAY RESERVE.	Jan. 1st.		Our Artillery saw the New Year in, but there was no reply from the enemy. We relieved the 19th R.W.F. in the Right Subsector. A & B in the front line, C & D in close support. Relief completed without incident at 8-30pm.	
BULLE-COURT.	Jan. 2nd.		Companies busy improving line, laying duckboards, wiring, and new dug-outs. Weather hard and frosty. Col. Benzie R. awarded Bar to his D.S.O. in NEW YEAR'S HONOURS LIST, and Major W.E. Brown, Bar to M.C. Draft of 75 reported.	
BULLE-COURT.	Jan. 3rd.		Enemy artillery much more active. Front system shelled intermittently throughout the day. Inter-Company relief carried through without incident. Draft of 100 posted to Battalion (Transfers from our 6th Pioneers).	
BULLE-COURT.	Jan. 4th.		Enemy artillery still active. GOLLIWOG TRENCH blown in in five places. No casualties. Capt. Lloyd proceeded on leave to U.K.	
BULLE-COURT.	Jan. 5th.		At 6-0am, three S.O.S's. put up on our right. Battalion stood to, but there was no infantry action on our front. Battalion relieved by the 19th R.W.F. and moved to NORTH CAMP, MORY. R.S.M. Vatcher returned from Leave from U.K. Relief completed 8-30pm without incident.	
MORY.	Jan. 6th.		Lt.Col. R. Benzie D.S.O. proceeded on leave to U.K. Church services held in morning. Major General J. Ponsonby inspected our lines.	
MORY.	Jan. 7th.		A & B Coys. for baths at MORY. Day spent in training, also Spit-Locking trench to represent DOG TRENCH to practice for upcoming Raid. Draft of 38 reported.	
MORY.	Jan. 8th.		C & D Coys. to MORY for Baths. 2/Lieuts. J.B. Greaves and Rogers Jones returned from leave. C.O. inspected last three New Drafts. Day extremely cold and rain and snow somewhat hampered training.	
BULLE-COURT.	Jan. 9th.		Capt. J.M.W. Barker proceeded on leave to U.K. 2/Lieut. Greaves took over duties as Acting Adjutant. We relieved the 19th R.W.F. in the Right Subsector. A & B in front line, C & D in close support. Relief completed at 8-35pm without incident.	

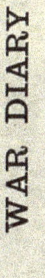

Army Form C. 2118.

(2)

WAR DIARY
or
INTELLIGENCE SUMMARY.
(Erase heading not required.)

Instructions regarding War Diaries and Intelligence Summaries are contained in F.S. Regs., Part II. and the Staff Manual respectively. Title pages will be prepared in manuscript.

Place	Date 1918	Hour	Summary of Events and Information	Remarks and references to Appendices
BULLE-COURT.	Jan. 10th.		This morning about 4-0am one of our listening patrols at about U21.b.25.40. saw two of the enemy advancing towards them. They allowed them to come on and then tried to cut them off. One of the enemy fired at patrol and succeeded in getting away, the other being captured and brought in to our lines. He belongs to the 453rd Regt. 11 Coy. and is a Pole. Name given as Pte. Winkler. The 'thaw' having set in the Companies were busy improving and clearing trenches. The night was quiet on the whole without anything of importance happening.	
BULLE-COURT.	Jan. 11th.		Day quiet. Intermittent shelling on both sides. Inter-Company relief carried out without incident by 7-45pm. C & D Coys. now in front line, A & B in close support. From 9-0pm we bombarded enemy lines with gas shells throughout the night. No retaliation. Ours and hostile machine guns very active all night. The Right Company sent out a Patrol of 2 officers and 4 O.R. to reconnoitre DOG TRENCH. As the wire was reached the Patrol were observed and were fired at with machine guns and rifle fire from DOG TRENCH. One of the Officers, 2nd/Lieut. J. Brewer being severely wounded. He was brought back to our lines under great difficulties owing to the intense darkness and sodden condition of the ground.	
BULLE-COURT.	Jan. 12th.		2nd/Lieut. J. Brewer reported to have died of wounds. Day and night exceptionally quiet.	
BULLE-COURT.	Jan. 13th.		At 4-30 this morning there was a heavy bombardment away on our left lasting for about an hour. Remainder of the day quiet. 2nd/Lieut. Chapman proceeded on a Lewis Gun course. The Battalion relieved by the 19th R.W.F. and moved to RAILWAY RESERVE. Relief completed by 7-30pm without incident.	
RAILWAY RESERVE.	Jan. 14th.		Battalion on R.E. fatigues, rivetting and repairing trenches. All quiet. 2/Lieut. Phillips proceeded on leave.	
RAILWAY RESERVE.	Jan. 15th.		50% all Coys. bathed at ST. LEGER. Heavy showers of rain. Trenches about knee deep in mud and water. Party for intended Raid on DOG TRENCH practising at NORTH CAMP, MORY, under 2nd/Lieuts. Pitten, Dilloway, and Capp. Lieut. Francis reported off leave.	

Army Form C. 2118.

WAR DIARY
or
INTELLIGENCE SUMMARY.
(Erase heading not required.)

Instructions regarding War Diaries and Intelligence Summaries are contained in F. S. Regs., Part II. and the Staff Manual respectively. Title pages will be prepared in manuscript.

Place	Date 1918.	Hour	Summary of Events and Information	Remarks and references to Appendices
RAILWAY RESERVE.	Jan. 16th.		Battalion all employed on working parties in trenches; the sudden thaw and heavy rain making them almost impassable - Men are continually having to be dug out of the mud, but do very good work. A Company being specially prominent. Remaining 50% to baths at ST. LEGER. Div. General G.O.C. & C.O. witnessed the raid practise.	
RAILWAY RESERVE.	Jan. 17th.		Battalion employed clearing communication trenches. 2nd/Lieuts. Dicks, Morgan, and Marshall joined for duty. Relieved 19th R.W.F. in the front line - completed 10-0pm without incident.	
BULLE-COURT.	Jan. 18th.		Raiding Party returned from ERVILLERS. The night passed quietly. During the day our guns shelled DOG TRENCH.	
BULLE-COURT.	Jan. 19th.		Trenches now quite impassable. The Posts have to be approached 'over the top' by night only. All Companies working hard to overcome this difficulty. Day and night very quiet.	
BULLE-COURT.	Jan. 20th.		Day and night exceptionally quiet.	
BULLE-COURT.	Jan. 21st.		Capt. H.C. Lloyd returned from Leave. Battalion relieved by the 19th R.W.F. and moved to NORTH CAMP, MORY. Relief completed by 8-15pm without incident.	
MORY.	Jan. 22nd.		Lieut. Col. R. Benzie D.S.O. returned from Leave. 2nd/Lieut. F. Eames proceeded on Leave. 2nd/Lieut. Loxton reported for duty. B. C. & D. Coys. for baths at MORY in the morning, A Coy. in the afternoon.	
MORY.	Jan. 23rd.		Capt. W.A.G.Foster proceeded on leave to U.K. Day spent in training and improving the Camp. During night working party of 1 Officer and 50 O.R. per Coy. provided for digging Defence Line near ECOUST.	
MORY.	Jan. 24th.		A. & C Coys. to baths at MORY for foot treatment during morning. B. & D. Coys. during the afternoon. Coys. busy improving the Camp, i.e. laying duck boards and erecting splinter proof screens around all huts.	

Army Form C. 2118.

WAR DIARY
or
INTELLIGENCE SUMMARY.
(Erase heading not required.)

Instructions regarding War Diaries and Intelligence Summaries are contained in F. S. Regs., Part II. and the Staff Manual respectively. Title pages will be prepared in manuscript.

Place	Date 1918.	Hour	Summary of Events and Information	Remarks and references to Appendices
MORY.	Jan. 25th.		Day spent in cleaning up Camp and preparing for the Line. Battalion relieved the 19th R.W.F. in the Right Subsector. A. & B. Coys. in the front line, C. & D. in close support. General Crozier proceeded on leave to U.K., Lt.Col. R. Benzie D.S.O. taking command of the Brigade. Major Brown M.C. to command the Battalion during Col. Benzie's absence. Very quiet. Bright moon made patrolling difficult. 2nd/Lieut. J.W. Capp slightly wounded whilst reconnoitring DOG TRENCH. Capt. J.M.W. Barker returned from leave, and took over the duties of Adjutant.	
BULLE- COURT.	Jan. 26th.		Major C.E. Jenkins left to take command of the 18th Battalion The Welsh Regiment. Coys. busy revetting posts and clearing trenches. VALLEY TRENCH now passable. Day and night exceptionally quiet.	
BULLE- COURT.	Jan. 27th.		Day very misty rendering observation impossible. The night was quiet the exception that about 8-9pm there was a lively bombardment on the Right Coy. Front Line lasting for half an hour.	
BULLE- COURT.	Jan. 28th.		Lt. F.W. Pozzi proceeded on leave to U.K. 2nd/Lieut. W. Giddams returned from Corps GAS Course. Day and night passed quietly.	
BULLE- COURT.	Jan. 29th.		2nd/Lieut. W.H. Pitten proceeded on leave. Day was quiet. In the evening Battalion was relieved by the 19th R.W.F. Relief was completed without incident by 8-0pm. Battalion then went into support. H.Q. AND A. & D. Coys. in RAILWAY RESERVE; B. Coy. in RAILWAY EMBANKMENT: C. Coy. in MAN SUPPORT.	
RAILWAY RESERVE.	Jan. 30th.		Whde Battalion had foot treatment at ST. LEDGER. At night all men worked on new communication trench from VALLEY TRENCH to Front Line.	
RAILWAY RESERVE.	Jan. 31st.		Weather very cloudy and misty. Throughout the day enemy shelled RAILWAY RESERVE with shrapnel and H.E. D Coy. had 10 O.R. wounded. At night all men again worked on new communication trench. Large batch of orders received regarding impending disbanding of the Battalion.	

W.J. Morton
Major
Commanding 12th Battalion South Wales Borderers.
31/1/18.

119th Brigade.

40th Division.

Battalion became part of 9th ENTRENCHING BATTALION

16.2.18.

12th BATTALION

SOUTH WALES BORDERERS

FEBRUARY 1918.

WAR DIARY or INTELLIGENCE SUMMARY

Army Form C. 2118.

12 SWB

Place	Date	Hour	Summary of Events and Information	Remarks and references to Appendices
Railway Reserve	1/2/18		Enemy again shelled Railway Ravine inflicting casualties but very few men were hit. All available men worked on new communication trench at night.	
"	2/2/18		Working parties in the morning under REs. In the evening we relieved the 1st S.W.B. in the right subsector. Relief was completed without incident by 8.30 pm.	
Bellecourt	3/2/18		A quiet day. Patrols from both companies out at night.	
"	4/2/18		Another quiet day. At night we attempted to raid Day trench. A party of 3 officers (2/Lt Dilloway R/ Little R/ Saxton) 5 NCO's & 28 other ranks left our line at 2 am 5/2/18 got into position by 3.15 a.m. next half of wire was cut through successfully but a second belt was then discovered about 10 yards nearer to the trench. Party went forward to cut the 2nd belt but as they were starting to do this the enemy put down a ground flare which showed the party up & they were greeted with a shower of bombs. 2/Lt Dilloway & one other rank were hit & several further attempts were made to cut the second belt but each time our men were seen & fired on and bombed. Eventually the party had no option but to retire. The whole party reached our line in safety. A little rain fell in the night made the trench rather dirty & slippery	
"	5/2/18		A quiet day & night.	

21X 3 sheets

WAR DIARY or INTELLIGENCE SUMMARY

Army Form C. 2118.

Place	Date	Hour	Summary of Events and Information	Remarks and references to Appendices
Bullecourt	6/2/18		A quiet day. In the evening we were relieved by 10th H.L.I. Relief was completed without incident by 9pm. 2/Lt R Taylor reported back from Brigade School. 2/Lt C Hart & 2/Lt J Pile, 2/Lt R Hamilton-Taylor & 2/Lt Chrislow reported as on leave. 2/Lt W Wilson took charge of transport during absence of transport officer.	JPG
Marcq	7/2/18 8/2/18		Day spent in cleaning up, putting huts in hab. Equipment left by 6.45am orderly room, stand to, stand to, stand to, men. #4 by Lt R Callahan. Stood down, cup through at 7-30am. Draft of 62 (L/Off & 61 O.R.s) (by Regn. S.O.) 50 men of Coy were inspected by the Adjutant O.C. 9th Bn (L/Cpl Cannis S.O.) during the morning left in the afternoon for 5th R.S.R.	JPG
"	9/2/18		Bn. parade in morning when bOlrcad scape Inam River Laugher laid etc Divl Genl Inspection orderly in the afternoon of the Bn. Nothing in of application equipment was correctly etc. Left W. factr 2/Lt J Bumes returned from leave. Capt M Brown O.C. Coy went on leave may. 2/Lt Jenkins proceeded on leave to UK.	JPG
Bellecourt	10/2/18		Battalion left Marcq by bus at 9am. for Bellacount arriving there about 11am all of Coys were successfully billeted by 1pm. We now had our all officers reconnoitred outer command of left pt came part of the left Brigade's support stood up Frontier D.Co. Hd. Quarters (Green M.Pt) Wilson strenched as relieved. No being attacked to personnel were left behind as under left tempo. the morning — the 1/21 E. Lancashire. 1st Bn 9/M.B.	JPG

WAR DIARY
INTELLIGENCE SUMMARY

Army Form C. 2118.

Place	Date	Hour	Summary of Events and Information	Remarks and references to Appendices
Bellacourt	11/3/18		2nd Bn. 5 Officers & 101 men. Major Morgan Owen, Pemberton, Capt. Pryor Jones & Lt. Kirkpatrick	
"	12/3/18		Training was devoted to training afternoon to games Matches (inter Platoon) until March 14 when gas mask inspection	
"	13/3/18		Preliminary orders for rehearsal of operation by Entrenching Bn. from the remains of 11 Corps & 17 Div at ? to 13th at 7.30 & to 10'.	
"	14		Arrangements were made and it will depend on weather by 10'	
"	15		Inter Platoon competition for skill at arms.	
"	16		Battalion moved to Bailleulmont where it became part of an Entrenching Group. Officers went with Bn., the Company Comdrs. and 1 Lt. Pryor kept with Pl. HQ of Pl. A.Sjt. Pl.Sjt. and Batmen 2/Lt. J.C. Crumbs 2/Lt. J. Bowie the Pl. Sjt. & Batman 2/Lt J Miller 2/Lt. J. Bowie the remainder of officers went to Base has no posting	

Kim Bowers
Capt.
for Major
Comdg 10th Bn Devonshires

www.ingramcontent.com/pod-product-compliance
Lightning Source LLC
Chambersburg PA
CBHW081535160426
43191CB00011B/1765